"WIN THE LOST AT ANY COST!"

Disconnected
and Don't Know It

GWATHNEY LEAK SR.

DISCONNECTED AND DON'T KNOW IT

Published by Lee's Press and Publishing Company
www.LeesPress.net

All rights reserved, Copyright 2019. Except for brief excerpts for review purposes, no part of this book may be reproduced or used in any form without written permission from Gwathney Leak Sr. and/or the publisher.

This document is published by Lee's Press and Publishing Company located in the United States of America. It is protected by the United States Copyright Act, all applicable state laws and international copyright laws. The information in this document is accurate to the best of the ability of Gwathney Leak Sr. at the time of writing. The content of this document is subject to change without notice.

ISBN 13: 978-1-7329441-4-5

CONTENTS

Dedication 1
The Cover Explanation... 2
Acknowledgments 3
Preface... 4
Introduction... 6
Disconnected and Don't Know It.. 17
Now Concerning the Calling of God 23
Women in Ministry... 44
Gender Roles in Marriage 59
Neither Male nor Female 63
The Position of the Man/The Position of the Woman 66
War In Heaven – The Garden of Eden................................ 79
Role Reversal 87
Role Reversal of the Man and the Woman 95
Men Are Out of Place 103
Power, Money, and Love.. 110
Modern Day Church 118
Marriage 125
I Wanna Be Something 132
Pastors and Leadership 139
Summary 151

DEDICATION

I dedicate this book to my daughter Tonya Yvonne Leak Vinson who encouraged me to write and publish this book. As I shared things with my daughter about the Bible and things that I experienced in ministry; she expressed I should write a book. For years she said, "Daddy why don't you write some of this stuff down? Just call me and let me write it down for you daddy." I would tell her how I couldn't write a book, but she told me that I had a book in me.

For four to five years she kept pushing me to write. I told her, "Tonya, I can't even type." And to that she said, "Call me and let me record it." I never followed through despite how she saw things in me. She saw things I didn't see in myself. I was like Jeremiah who talked about what he could not do. I was looking at my inability and she was telling me like God told Jeremiah, "Don't say what you can't do." She reminded me of what I preached and told others many times, and for this reason, I dedicate this book to her.

Tonya Yvonne Leak Vinson
March 1, 1971 – November 5, 2017

THE COVER EXPLANATION

Therefore, say thou unto them, Thus saith the Lord of host; Turn ye unto me, saith the Lord of hosts, and I will turn unto you, saith the Lord of hosts.

Zechariah 1:3

The cover design symbolizes the disconnection man has from the assignment of God. The Church, as we know it, is lost. Much like the Rich Young Ruler in *Matthew 19:21* where Jesus tells him to sell everything he had and give to the poor before following him, God says the same to every member of the Church. The man sitting on the bench as well as the image of a man above him displays the dilemma of being lost, alone, and disconnected.

Every member of the Lord's Church must ask the question, "How did I get here? Was it the things I've said, thought, believed, or done? We must ask and answer these questions before we can discover how to get out of the mess we've created. Our connection can only occur when we commit to changing what we say, think, believe and do, and realign ourselves with the Word of God. Refuse to receive the Word and not retain it. *Mark 4:14*

Connect or reconnect to God!

ACKNOWLEDGEMENTS

I acknowledge my daughter Monica McKinnie who has supported me throughout this process. Thank you for spending quality time and listening as I discussed this book with you. I thank God for you, and I love you very much.

To my assistant, Louise Warren, I acknowledge your administrative support and assistance in the collection and organizing of my personal stories, teachings, and ministry experiences. Translating, typing, emailing, and organizing meetings has contributed immensely to the development of *Disconnected and Don't Even Know It*. With God, all things are possible.

Thank you both!

PREFACE

There's a difference between a church and a congregation. Anybody can be in a congregation, but everyone is not in the church. The church is a body of people who are saved, baptized and filled with the Holy Spirit. I encourage you to read the book of Acts for this is the beginning of the Church (Acts 2:38.) Peter told those present to repent and be baptized "Every one of you in the name of Jesus Christ for the remission of sins." He told them they would receive the gift of the Holy Ghost.

You may have a huge following, have pockets filled with money and fine cars. You may have armor-bearers, multiple churches, and your congregation may hang on every word you say as you travel from one church to the other. But you have allowed people to call you something that God hasn't: Bishop, Apostle, Doctor, Pastor, Evangelist, or First Lady. You appear to be successful, but this doesn't mean God called you to these titles. There are many churches that are successful according to world standards, but this is not so according to God's standard. These successes do not mean they are right. I say, you can be successful doing the wrong things!

Matthias was chosen by the eleven disciples, but you never hear about him again. Nor do you read that he was ever called by God, but by men. For some, what I will say will not be comprehensible. Some have conformed to the way of the world and have a deaf ear to the truth of God's Holy Word. I challenge anyone to approach me, not according to your opinion, but according to what scripture teaches. As Christians, we should be able to show people, by scripture, exactly where we are speaking from.

I Thessalonians 5: 21: *Prove all things; hold fast that which is good.*

II Timothy 3:16: *All scripture is given by inspiration of God, and is profitable for doctrine, for reproof, for correction, for instruction in righteousness.*

INTRODUCTION

Jesus said, the spirit of the Lord is upon Me, because He hath anointed Me to preach the gospel to the poor; He hath sent Me to heal the brokenhearted, to preach deliverance to the captives, and recovering of sight to the blind, to set at liberty them that are bruised. To preach the acceptable year of the Lord. Luke 4:18, 19

As Jesus knew His assignment, we as believers need to know what our assignment is as well. Every believer is sent with an assignment, and when you walk in that assignment, you walk in His name not yours. As I understood my assignments, my gifts caused the anointing of God in my life to come forward. Death is not the saddest thing that can happen to us. The saddest is to come to the earth and never fulfill your assignment. It may not be preaching, but you have to learn and understand what that assignment is.

My name is Gwathney Leak and I have Pastored five churches in my life time. I was saved from sin at the age of twenty-four. When God saved me, I wanted to do right. I remember asking God, just praying, "Lord if you are up there and you're real please save me." I was tired of the way I was living. God did it! He began to cleanse me. Now, I didn't stop doing everything at one time, but I stopped drinking, smoking, using drugs and cursing. I used to play basketball every Sunday and there was so much profanity being used. One Sunday one of the fellas said, "Hey Gwat, you ain't cursing no more?" I hadn't even paid any attention to this fact. I asked the Lord to forgive me and if he would let me get out of there that Sunday, I would never come back on Sunday again. He did and I never played basketball on Sunday again.

Before I got saved, if you cursed me out, those were fighting words. I meant that! But when God saved me, I didn't want to fight anymore. I rejoiced about it. I began realizing God had really changed my life. I found out that the more I began to walk in the things of God, the more persecution came. I was a threat to the devil. I didn't just want to preach, I wanted to be a threat to the devil. When I was a pastor, I told the people when I get up in the morning the devil says, "Oh, oh he's getting up!" He assigned demons to me. It reminds me of the gazelle and the lion: Every day the gazelle wakes up running because he knows he is the lion's favorite meal. As believers, we should wake up every day running for the Lord. I knew what it was like to be a sinner. I had done that all my life. But I got tired of the way I was living, and I asked God to save me.

There were many times I would go to church and was asked, "Why don't you come sit in the pulpit?" I didn't know you could sit up there; I didn't really care. But again, I was preaching for about six months without knowing I was a preacher. I was told I was a preacher, but the only thing I knew was I had a strong desire to go out and tell others about Jesus Christ. Mind you, I wasn't saved, so when God saved me, the only thing I knew was to tell people about Jesus Christ. They called it preaching. I asked, "Is that what you call this?" I didn't know because I didn't have any spiritual overtones. I didn't understand. I just wanted to share Christ with others. Then when they told me, "You're a preacher," I said, "Oh, okay that's what I am? I'm glad you let me know! I didn't know what I was. Just like God told Ananias, *"Arise, and go into the street which is called Straight and enquire in the house of Judas for one called Saul, of Tarsus: for, behold, he prayeth." Acts 9:11*

God told me to find a man named Charlie Clemmons. When I started with him, he taught me how to do things. I submitted to him and he taught me a lot. We would be on the streets everyday preaching the gospel. There was a group of us: men and women, laborers. On one occasion we were in downtown Winston-Salem, NC during the time when there was a lot of racial tension – a lot of prejudice. We were laying hands on people, black and white, and they were going out in the spirit. A white woman went out under the anointing of God. We prayed, "Lord, get her up Lord! Raise this white woman up before the police comes," She finally got up and we said, "THANK YOU JESUS!" I didn't have a Biblical knowledge, but I was connected to God. I didn't know it then, but I do now.

I cared about people and I wanted to see people saved. I was connected to God and I didn't know it. I didn't know why I wanted to do right by people. I was connected to God and He changed me. I knew something was happening to me, but I did not fully understand it all. He changed my heart. The Lord let me know that He had called me to preach His word. The Spirit of the Lord came to me and said, "Preach My Word," and from that day I began to study the Word of God. I told the Lord that whatever He told me to say I would say. I wouldn't be afraid; I would not be quiet!

Matthew 10:34-38 *Think not that I am come to send peace on earth. I came not to send peace, but a sword.*

For I am come to set a man at variance against his father, and the daughter against her mother, and the daughter-in-law against her mother-in-law.

And a man's foes shall be they of his own household.

He that loveth father or mother more than me is not worthy of me: and he that loveth son or daughter more than me is not worthy of me.

And he that taketh not his cross, and followeth after me, is not worthy of me. **Matthew 10:34-38**

Paul writes in *Galatians 1:12, I neither received it of man, neither was I taught it, but by the revelation of Jesus Christ.* Woe unto me if I preach not the gospel. The Men of God, Pastors, Prophets, Apostles and Bishops need to stand up. We have to say some hard things, but we have to always tell people the truth according to what the Bible says. We can't just tell truth to some people and not tell it to all – even to your own family. The truth is not just for everybody else and not your own family, wife and children.

Isaiah 58:1 states: *"Cry aloud, spare not, lift up thy voice like a trumpet, and show my people their transgression, and the house of Jacob their sins."* I've lost a lot, but I haven't truly lost anything because I'm still connected to God. And I know it. When God called me to preach, I presented my body to Christ as a living sacrifice. I was on the street preaching six days a week. Night and day, I was there because He called me to do it. I wasn't a member of anybody's church when I started. Eventually, I joined a church about six months after I got saved.

If God called you to preach, you have to do it, and you don't have to get permission. God called you. I had a strong anointing on me to go out and preach the gospel. I was on the streets preaching to whites, blacks and anybody who would listen. I was committed to the things God had assigned to me. And I was secure about who God created me to be. I was excited about doing something good. I remember one day a man cursed me out because I was sharing with him about how Christ changed my life. He could change his also, but the man cursed me out. Before I got saved I was a hell raiser and I wouldn't take that then. This man knew it, and he would have never stood in my face and said what he said before I got saved. He knew he would have been in trouble.

He realized that something had happened to me because I didn't look or respond the same. I knew God had saved me and I got excited. I got excited because I was being cursed out for doing something good. Hallelujah! Thank you, Jesus! I got cursed out for telling somebody about Jesus! People began saying I had gone crazy!

I began running revival in the streets and it began to

affect other brothers in the church that were preaching. I was committed to the call of God on my life. Pastors wanted to give me evangelistic license. I didn't know anything about evangelistic license. My response was, "Will it make me preach better?" The Pastor said, "No, I'm not saying it's going to make you preach better." I told him, "then I'm fine with what I have." If it was not going to make me do better or be better, I was fine. I turned down stuff like that. By stuff, I mean titles and popularity. I had a name before I got saved. My reputation preceded me: The judges knew me. I didn't get saved to be popular, people knew my name. The police knew my name – I had done so much mess! I was very secure about the calling of God on my life.

God had prepared me all my life. When I would go to church, I never desired to sit in the pulpit. I wanted to sit in the audience because there I could testify. I didn't care anything about sitting in a pulpit. It was like the integration thing (white's and black's bathrooms.) Both were bathrooms. The key is not where you sit, but is God sitting with you?

When people called and asked me to come and preach or run a revival, they would ask me how much I charged? I said, "I don't charge you anything." How could I charge for something that didn't belong to me? I'm not saying that people didn't do things for me, but what I'm saying is that it was not a requirement for people to do something for me in return. Even when I went out of town it was the same thought: I went without charge. I never put a demand on anybody. To this day, I have never asked the church for a raise. If they did something, that was between them and

God. But I never asked or put a demand on anyone. Many times, when they gave me something, I gave it back.

I was excited to be a messenger. I just wanted to do whatever would make a difference. I went without charging because God called me. I never put a demand on anybody to give me anything. When I came to the church, I came with a message. The Holy Spirit taught me. It was about winning souls and telling people about what He had done for me. God changed my life and I had a hunger and thirst to know more about Him. I wanted to know how to win souls for the Kingdom of God. The Gospel is for lost people. The scriptures say, *"Then saith he unto his disciples, the harvest truly is plenteous, but the laborers are few; Pray ye therefore the Lord of the harvest, that he will send forth laborers into his harvest." Matthew 9:37-38*

I put in my application. I prayed and I studied the Word. I wanted to show God He could trust me. I began reading the first four Gospels over and over again. I read them for months. I didn't want to tell anybody anything wrong (that's why I didn't just read, I studied the Bible.) I wanted to know about Jesus: who He was and what He did. What was His purpose in coming? If I could understand Him, I could understand my assignment. Because the Bible states, *"Let this mind be in you, which was also in Christ Jesus." Philippians 2:5* I started doing it! I'd go downtown every day before I went to work. Many times, I would go after I got off work too. I'd go again and again.

In Winston-Salem there was a place called the Dungeon, and a group of us went there to preach. On one occasion, there was a man who told me to shut up. Now, I hadn't been saved long, and again, before I accepted Christ I wouldn't take that kind of stuff. The Spirit of the Lord told me to be quiet, so I didn't say anything. Another brother said, "Gwat he doesn't want to hear you but we do" My response was, "We won't preach to you tonight, but we will pray for you." People started going out under the anointing and power of God. We were in front of a club where people were drinking and smoking. The unbelievers began to experience the manifestation of the Holy Spirit, and the power of God moved during that time like I'd never seen before.

    I thank God for those I was with that night. I learned from them. They encouraged me like Brother Charlie Clemmons beforehand. God anointed me to preach the Gospel, and I prayed as David prayed in *Psalm 51:10: Create in me a clean heart, O God; and renew a right spirit within me.* God gave me a clean heart and renewed a right spirit in me. In my lifetime of ministry, I have never asked anybody if I could preach at their church. I've never asked anybody to pastor a church. I told God that if He called me to preach it was His responsibility to open those doors, and He proved it to be so.

    I was constantly trying to show God that He could trust me. That was my main objective. It wasn't about me. Everything I did, God opened the door for me to do it. People call me now, even in my seventies, and He is still doing it. Glory to God; Praise His Holy name! I should never have to ask anybody to preach at their church. I've heard about and know preachers who send resumes to churches. But I have never sent a resume to any church. Every preacher ought to understand that if God calls you it's His responsibility to send you. Why would you get upset and angry when a church chooses another pastor instead of you? If God wanted you there, you would be there.

I was saved at the age of twenty-four, but I did not begin the pastorate until I was about thirty-seven. Remember, He said, *"And I will give you pastors according to mine heart, which shall feed you with knowledge and understanding." Jeremiah 3:15* The Lord also said, *"And he gave some, apostles; and some, prophets; and some, evangelist; and some, pastors and teachers; For the perfecting of the saints, for the work of the ministry, for the edifying of the body of Christ: Till we all come in the unity of the faith, and of the knowledge of the Son of God, unto a perfect man, unto the measure of the stature of the fullness of Christ." Ephesians 4:11-13* But don't stop reading because Paul continues to say, *"That we henceforth be no more children, tossed to and fro, and carried about with every wind of doctrine, by the sleight of men, and cunning craftiness whereby they lie in wait to deceive;" Ephesians 4:14*... Aw man, it's all good!

We've lost sight... This is not about us but it's about what God has called us to. When Satan comes at you he knows what you like. It is a sad commentary when a pastor becomes a millionaire and stands before the people like gain is godliness. I think it's a lie from hell when a pastor leads his people to believe that the more they have materialistically, the closer they are to God. The Bible says, *"For what shall it profit a man, if he shall gain the whole world and lose his soul? Or what shall a man give in exchange for his soul?" Mark 8:36-37* The Bible also state: *"My people are destroyed for the lack of knowledge:" Hosea 4:6a*

These are some of the devices Satan uses to disconnect believers from God. We get too involved with our education and status. As a pastor, I have to be careful how I use my position. We are leaders and people are watching us. Many leaders use their position to manipulate, deceive, trick and even pimp for gainsaying. God doesn't have anything to do with this. Satan's main objective is to disconnect God's people from His Word. What does Satan know about you that you have forgotten about you? One thing Satan knows is you have creative words inside you. If he can get you to disconnect from God's word you're defeated. There's nothing wrong with having money but when the money has you it will mess you up.

Satan will come to you just like he did to Jesus. He comes to distract you, and if he can get you with the money, then that's the way he's coming. *Matthew 12:34-35, 37 says, O generation of viper, how can ye, being evil, speak good things? For out of the abundance of the heart the mouth speaketh. A good man out of the good treasure of the heart bringeth forth good things: and an evil man out of the evil treasure bringeth forth evil things. For by thy word thou shalt be justified, and by thy words thou shalt be condemned.*

Lucifer wasn't originally known as the devil, but he was an

anointed Cherub in the presence of God. He wanted to ascend into heaven and exalt his throne above the stars of God. Like many today, he looked at himself and wanted to be like The Most High God. He was so influential that he convinced a third of the angels to rebel against God. Imagine, they were in the presence of God and he was able to persuade a third of the angels to follow him. Because of his deception, they, along with Lucifer were kicked out of heaven. The Bible says woe, unto the inhabitants of the earth for Satan has come down with great wrath. No wonder why we are going through what we go through now. Satan has not changed, he's still working. We're DISCONNECTED AND DON'T EVEN KNOW IT!

DISCONNECTED AND DON'T KNOW IT

I've made many mistakes throughout my lifetime, which includes decisions during my time in the ministry. One specifically relates to men and women in ministry. These decisions were made out of emotions, feelings, and what I thought best. This is how many people operate today. I had a woman ask about women preachers. And so, I've done some studying within the scriptures to see what the Bible says. When this sister asked me this question it caused me to think, because I didn't want to cause anyone to go to hell because of wrong teaching or misinterpretation of the scriptures. As Christians, we should say what the scriptures say and not what we feel or think. II Peter 1:20 says, *"Knowing this first, that no prophecy of the scripture is of any private interpretation."* We should not add our own private interpretation of what the scriptures plainly states. To do this makes us liars.

Proverbs 30:6 *Add thou not unto His words, lest he reprove thee, and thou be found a liar.*

Deuteronomy 4:2 *Ye shall not add unto the word which I command you, neither shall ye diminish aught from it, that ye may keep the commandments of the Lord your God which I command you.*

I have searched scriptures to find the truth as it pertains to *women* and *men,* and each of their roles in the church. The scripture supports the fact that God uses women so there is no doubt in my mind that God uses many women. What I have found thus far is that there is a distinct difference in the role between men and women. Again, I say, as it concerns the church.

Contrary to what many may believe, as I ask the questions, make statements, while searching the scriptures, nothing supports what we've accepted in ordaining and licensing women to pastor, preach, evangelize, and consecrating them to the bishopric and apostleship. It is not my desire in any way to put women down, but to know the truth and teach others as the Holy Spirit reveals, I'm in search of scripture that *support* the fact that God uses women in the same capacity as He uses men – only as it pertains to His church (the Body of Christ). My opinion or personal thoughts are not relevant, only what scripture teaches. I have found that people get angry and upset with me when I ask them to support what they say scripturally.

We, as Christians, should say only what lines up with what scripture says. Anything that anyone says contrary to what scripture teaches is a liar. We have interjected so many of our own thoughts, opinions and feelings into what the Word of God says that we no longer recognize the truth of God's Word. We've added things according to our feelings, or to what others have accepted around us, and even conformed to the ways of the world.

2 Timothy 2:15 *Study to show thyself approved unto God, a workman that needeth not to be ashamed, rightly dividing the word of truth.*

We have an obligation to God and the people of God to rightly divide the Word and stay away from our feelings or what we think. We should stay away from what our friends, family, colleagues and peers say. If we can't say scripturally what is written, we should be silent. When the Bible is silent, we should be silent.

In my study of God's Word I have found that God is a God of order.

God's Divine Order

1. God
2. Marriage
3. Family
4. Church
5. Government

Ephesians 1:22 *And hath put all things under his feet, and gave him to be the head over all things to the church.*

I Corinthians 11:3 *But I would have you know, that the head of every man is Christ; and the head of the woman is the man; and the head of Christ is God.*

Why would God give us an order in the home and change the order of His church? An excellent example is in Genesis 3:1-7 when He put the man in place. God gave man instructions in the Garden of Eden, not the woman. After the woman hearkened unto the voice of Satan, she gave also to her husband with her and he did eat, their eyes were opened. In verse 8 you see that they both heard the voice of the Lord God, but God called to Adam, not Eve, as

He walked in through the garden in the cool of the day. Why did God not call out to Adam and Eve? Because He held Adam accountable; not Eve. God put Adam in charge.

When Adam submitted and hearkened to the voice of his wife, he disobeyed God. This is what many men, husbands and pastors do today. It's not wrong to listen to your wife but if God has told you what to do, you should always do what God says. You don't have to get any one's permission to do what God instructs you to do. Again, I say, *God is a God of order!* Man would not write something in scripture to say something he could not do. He would not lock himself up or make rules about things he could not do. This would back him up in a corner... Let me say again, *God is a God of Order.*

I Corinthians 14:33-38 *For God is not the author of confusion, but of peace, as in all churches of the saints.*

Let your women keep silence in the churches; for it is not permitted unto them to speak; but they are commanded to be under obedience, as also saith the law.

And if they will learn anything, let them ask their husbands at home: for it is a shame for women to speak in the church.

What? Came the word of God out from you? Or came it unto you only?

If any man thinks himself to be a prophet, or spiritual, let him acknowledge that the things that I write unto you are the commandments of the Lord.

But if any man be ignorant, let him be ignorant.

This is not just Paul's opinion, it's the Lord's command. Paul is not saying that women can't worship or praise in the church. There had to be some other things going on. Here, Paul was speaking to a specific situation: The church was conducting business and Paul was telling the women to wait until they get home and ask their husbands. Even if you didn't have a husband, then your pastor, a brother (who was saved; filled with the Holy Ghost, Spirit–led) should be able to answer questions you had. Not any man, but a man who was living and governing himself by the Word of God – by the Holy Spirit. A man who had spiritual character and integrity.

God does not contradict His Word. If a woman was unable to speak in the church, she couldn't pray or prophesy? If we take what is said here literally, it would mean that women are not allowed to speak in church; Not respond when the pastor asks for comments or questions from the audience. Why would Paul in I Corinthians 11 speak of women praying or prophesying if they had the appropriate attire? (Paul said previously that women should wear a head covering when they pray and prophesy.) This is why the Bible says, *Study to shew thyself approved unto God, a workman that needeth not to be ashamed, rightly dividing the word of truth. II Timothy 2:15*

We study to know why things are being said, while being careful not to change the meaning of what is being said. (Reference *II Timothy 3:16*) In other words, we don't have to rewrite or interpret what has already been done by holy men of God as they were moved by the Holy Ghost. When the Word is silent you be silent.

NOW CONCERNING THE CALLING OF GOD

I have been preaching for more than 40 years and the majority of people, both men and women, who say God called them to preach, always equate a desire to serve God with preaching. Every person God call is also given an assignment. Listen to the words of Apostle Paul. *Paul, an apostle of Jesus Christ by the will of God, according to the promise of life which is in Christ Jesus.* Paul was *called* to be an apostle. Jesus said, *The Spirit of the Lord is upon me, because He hath anointed me to preach the gospel to the poor; he hath sent me to heal the brokenhearted, to preach deliverance to the captives, and recovering of sight to the blind, to set at liberty them that are bruised, Luke 4:18*

In Exodus 3, God called Moses to lead His people. When God calls us, he gives each of us an assignment and purpose to fulfill. As we see with the Prophet Jeremiah, the scripture says, *Before I formed thee in the belly, I knew thee; and before thou camest forth out of the womb I sanctified thee, and I ordained thee a prophet unto the nations. Jeremiah 1:5* God also says to the prophet, *For I know the thoughts that I think toward you, saith the Lord, thoughts of peace, and not of evil, to give you an expected end. Jeremiah 29:11*

The Apostle Paul taught, *Having then gifts differing according to the grace that is given us, whether prophecy, let us prophesy according to the proportion of faith; Or ministry, let us wait on our ministering: or he that teacheth, on teaching; Or he that exhorteth, on exhortation: he that giveth, let him do it with simplicity; he that ruleth, with diligence,; he that sheweth mercy, with cheerfulness. Roman 12:6-8* Yet, everybody wants to preach.

When reading the book of Revelation, God reproved every church except one. He told one, *Nevertheless I have somewhat against thee, because thou hast left thy first love. Revelation 2:4*. He told another one, *I know thy works, that thou hast a name that thou livest, and art dead. Revelation 3:1b* He told the church at Philadelphia, *I know thy works: behold I have set before thee an open door, and no man can shut it: for thou hast a little strength, and hast kept my word, and hast not denied my name. Revelation 3:8* He told the church at Laodicea, *I know thou works, that thou are neither cold nor hot: I would thou wert cold or hot. So then because thou are lukewarm, and neither cold or hot, I will spew thee out of my mouth. Revelation 3:15*

He told the church at Smyrna, *I know thy works, and tribulation, and poverty, (but thou art rich) and I know the blasphemy of them which say they are Jews, and are not, but are the synagogue of Satan. Revelation 2:9* He said to the church at Pergamos, *I know thy works, and where thou dwelleth, even where Satan's seat is: and thou holdest fast my name, and hast not denied my faith, even in those days wherein Antipas was my faithful martyr, who was slain among you, where Satan dwelleth. Revelation 2:13* Some of these churches were successful but God had something against them. It wasn't that they weren't successful, but God said I have somewhat against you because you're doing something, I did not tell you to do. So, it is possible to do something He didn't tell you to do. To every preacher, pastor, apostle and bishop God has called, I strongly encourage you, whenever you tell someone to do something, make sure you show them what the Bible says. Because the Bible says that by His Word you are going to be justified and by it you will be condemned. I didn't write it. And again, I say, you can be successful doing something God didn't call you to do.

Think about it... What does God have against you? How can you endorse teaching God never taught? What we're dealing with is a lot of denominational teaching that's not scriptural. Jesus said, I'm going away but I will come again and receive you unto myself that where I am there you may be also. *John 14:3* Remember, Pastors and leaders were left in charge of the church. Look at His church. Will He be able to recognize His church when He returns? Some of the churches look like the ones in Revelation. He had something against every last one of them except one. What will He say to you when He returns?

Parishioners are not your people, they're God's people. He called you to train his people; teach them how to be disciples. Are you teaching them how to do programs and church stuff, or are you teaching them to be the church? It's up to you. The reason things have gotten so far off is because most are not saying anything. The gifts God left for the church was for the perfecting of the Saints. If you are perfecting God's people you work for Him. They are not your people; it is not your church. The church belongs to God. So, if you are working for Him, He told you to make disciples of His people.

Many are making congregational members and not disciples. If you were making disciples, you would be working outside of your church. It would be a wonderful thing if on Sundays, instead of going to church, the church would go into areas of the community to do ministry - loving on people. God set each member in His church according to *I Corinthians 12:27. And God hath set some in the church, first apostles, secondarily prophets, thirdly teachers, after that miracles, then gifts of healings, helps, governments, diversities of tongues. I Corinthians 12:28* It goes on to ask further questions, *Are all apostles? Are all prophets? Are all teachers? Are all workers of miracles? Have all the gifts of healing? Do all speak with tongues? Do all interpret?*

Look at this closely. Correct me if I'm wrong. When did God set a First Lady in place in the church? I know there are First Ladies in the White House; the president's wife became more visible at the turn of the 20th century. Public acknowledgement and importance of the role have grown over time. But, the title "First Lady" has become a role of distinction bestowed on current and former ladies of the White House. The first documented reference to a First Lady belongs to Martha Washington. She was referred to as Lady Washington, while George Washington was leading the Continental Army, and the term stayed with her after he was elected President. In 1849 our 12th U.S. President, Zachary Taylor used the expression "truly the first lady" while reciting a eulogy allegedly written by him in reference to Dolley Madison.

When President Taylor did her eulogy, he referred to her as dead lady because it was her funeral. So, when they call you First Lady what are people calling you? (Just THINK!) We use terminologies and things that we don't even know where these terms come from. The terminology refers to a dead lady. If you really want to know who the First Lady was read the second chapter of Genesis. According to the Bible, *And the Lord God caused a deep sleep to fall upon Adam, and he slept: and He took one of his ribs, and closed up the flesh instead thereof; And the rib, which the Lord God had taken from man, made he a woman, and brought her unto the man. And Adam said, this is now bone of my bones, and flesh of my flesh: she shall be called Woman, because she was taken out of Man. Genesis 2:21-23*

My brothers and sisters, according to the scripture, I present to you Eve, the first lady. This title was originated from our government institution and made its way into the church. But it is not a position or title from God to His church. First Lady and Co-Pastor is not in the Bible. I went to a church and there was a lady there which everyone addressed as First Lady. I went up to her and told her she had a unique name like mine. I said, my name is Gwathney, and you don't find many people with that name, just like yours – First. She said, "Oh, no. No, my name is not First. Then she told me her name. Why would you let someone call you by a name that is not yours? Your name is not "Pastor." Your name is not "Bishop." And it is not even "Evangelist."

There are some who won't even answer you if they are not recognized or referred to by their title-name. That is crazy! And we wonder why we are jacked up. The Bible tells us how to address one another. He said call the older women mothers, and the younger women sisters. Women, if you want to know what your title is look in *Titus 2:1-5.* Women have been called to teach the young women to be sober, to love their husbands; love their children. They have been called to be discreet, chaste, keepers at home; to be good. I know some women don't like to hear it, but Paul who was a chosen vessel by God tells us here, that a woman is to be obedient to their own husbands that the word of God be not blasphemed. I didn't write it; but Paul did. And we can't take the Word of God apart and use that which we like.

God's word doesn't change for anyone. The scripture states, *Jesus Christ the same yesterday, and today, and forever. Hebrews 13:8 Jesus said, Heaven and earth shall pass away, but my words shall not pass away. Matthew 24:35* He also said, *For verily I say unto you, Till heaven and earth pass, one jot or one tittle shall in no wise pass from the law, till all be fulfilled. Matthew 5:18* There are many other gifts in the Bible, but many men and women equate gifting to preaching. In Matthew 25, Christ speaks about being hungry, and ye gave Me meat: feeding the homeless and hungry, and visiting those hospitalized and imprisoned. But most always says, God called me to preach but they never preach.

Men and women sit in church Sunday after Sunday.

There are many gifts, but most want to preach. They don't do anything but sit in the pulpit and wait for somebody to ask them to preach. If you haven't preached anywhere in over a year, you need to turn your license in. I Corinthians 12:1-31 Many have been placed in positions that God did not call them to. Grandparents have said, "You look like a preacher." Others have been told by their wives, "Honey, you look like you got a call on your life." In the church, people will tell you that you must be a preacher because, "You sure sound like a preacher." Some pastors call their wives to be pastors; others go to school to become preachers. Some go to school so they can become a Pastor as their profession, but God didn't call them.

If you really want to know if you are a preacher read Luke 4:18-19 where Jesus tells us about His calling and who anointed Him to preach. Remember, after Judas betrayed Jesus he went and hanged himself. The slot for the 12th disciple became vacant, and the disciples appointed two men: Joseph, surnamed Justus, and Matthias to succeed him. The disciples prayed to the Lord and gave their lots. The lot fell upon Matthias and he was numbered with the eleven apostles. However, God had another plan. He chose Saul while he travelled to Damascus to bring men and women bound to Jerusalem.

In Acts 9:15 Jesus says, Go thy way: for he is a chosen vessel unto me, to bear my name before the Gentiles, and kings, and the children of Israel. God called Saul, not the disciples, nor his grandma or his buddies. Just because you appear successful, have a big church filled with people every Sunday, and are known as Pastor or Founder of your church, it does not mean God called you. Christ says, *And I say also unto thee, That thou art Peter, and upon this rock I will build my church; and the gates of hell shall not prevail against it. Matthew 16:18* Christ builds His church; He sets His members in place. Read in Ephesians 4. Each of us are given gifts for the perfecting of the saints, for the work of the ministry, for the edifying of the body of Christ.

I say again, too many equate their calling to *PREACHING*. This is not about women not being called, appointed, or chosen by God to pastor a church. Or to preach, be an apostle, bishop or evangelist. But this applies to anyone; man, woman, boy, or girl who is leading in the Lord's church without being called, appointed, or chosen by God. There is a difference between the church and its congregation. Anyone can reside within the congregation, but everyone is not enlisted in the church of Our Lord. The church is a body of people who are saved, baptized and filled with the Holy Spirit. I encourage you to read the book of Acts. The beginning of the Church can be discovered in Acts 2:38. *Then Peter said unto them, Repent, and be baptized every one of you in the name of Jesus Christ for the remission of sins, and ye shall receive the gift of the Holy Ghost.*

Brother Lewis Hunter and Gwathney Leak praying for the children.

Gwathney Leak and Charlie Clemmons: My mentor just finished preaching downtown Winston-Salem, NC.

Preaching at Mars Hill Baptist Church. I'll never forget quite a few people got saved that day.

The move of Ged in Happy Hill Garden. Having a joyous time!

Ministering in Happy Hill Garden.

Team Members proclaiming God's word on the streets of Winston-Salem, NC.

Gwathney Leak at twenty-four years. "I'm on my way."

Gwathney Leak preaching the gospel at Sandy Ridge Prison.

My ordination service at Powerhouse of Deliverance at age 26.

The move of the Holy Ghost on the streets of Winston-Salem, NC.

Gwathney Leak being welcomed in the Body of Christ.

Celebrating the anointing of God in Brother Charlie Clemmons' life. (His ordination service.) My friend and mentor.

Sharing Christ in Happy Hill Garden.

Children asking Brother Lewis Hunter for prayer.

The gathering and move of God in Happy Hill Garden,

The Men of Distinction and Daughters of Destiny mentoring program serving at Peachtree Middle.

Gwathney Leak at age twenty-seven. "Trying to find my way."

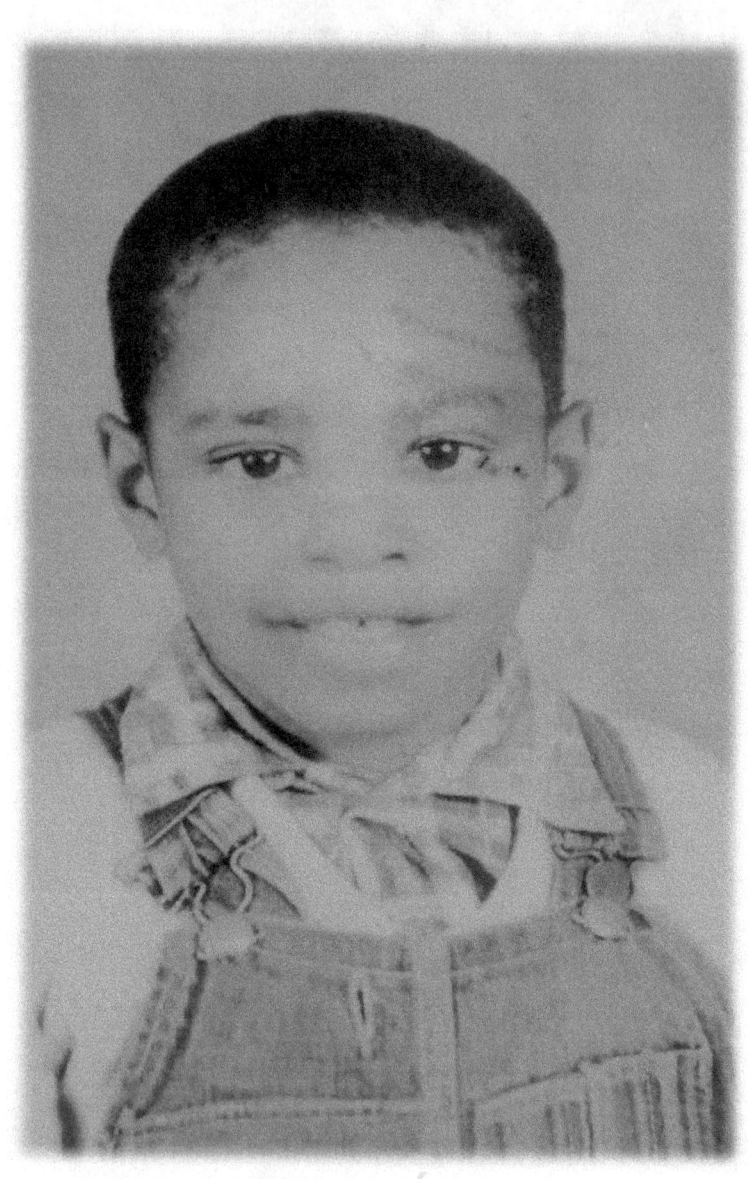
Gwathney Leak at age five. I didn't have a clue.

Tonya, the reason for this book; Jade, granddaughter; Gwathney Leak; and Monica, daughter and legal advisor.

WOMEN IN MINISTRY

Just a Few Things That Men and Women Have Misinterpreted

Many people say Mary was the first woman that carried the Word, but I say that's not true. The Bible said when the revelation came to her, the angel Gabriel spoke to her and said she was highly favored. He told her the Lord was with her and that she was blessed among women. The Bible said she was going to conceive in her womb and bring forth a son and call His name JESUS. She'd have a child, a son, not a Word. He told her the child's name – "His name shall be called Jesus." So, she didn't carry the Word. The Bible says, therefore also that holy thing which shall be born of thee shall be called the Son of God. She carried a baby for nine months. So, that's something else that should not be said. She did not carry the Word. Now, when He came He brought the Word. (Luke 1:26-35)

If the scriptures do not say she carried the Word and you say she carried the Word you're telling a lie. The scripture plainly says she carried a son and His name was Jesus. Yet, some people use this scripture to justify women preachers. They say if God used Mary to carry the Word, then he can use me to carry His Word too. We can't state something that God didn't. We can't change the Word to fit what we need it to say. He warns us not to add or take away from the Word. *Ye shall not add unto the word which*

I command you, neither shall ye diminish ought from it, that ye may keep the commandments of the LORD your God which I command you. Deuteronomy 4:2

Another misquoted scripture is when the woman of Samaria came to the well and Jesus asked her for a drink. He began to minister to her by saying the following, *There cometh a woman of Samaria to draw water: Jesus saith unto her Give me to drink. John 4:7* (Read the story in its entirety.) The woman left her water pot, and went her way into the city saying, *Come, see a man, which told me all things that ever I did: is not this the Christ? Then they went out of the city, and came unto him. John 4:29-30. And many of the Samaritans of that city believed on him for the saying of the woman, which testified, He told me all that ever I did. So when the Samaritans were come unto him, they besought him that he would tarry with them: and he abode there two days. And many more believed because of his own word. And said unto the woman, Now we believe, not because of thy saying: for we have heard him ourselves, and know that this is indeed the Christ, the Savior of the world. John 4:39-42*

This story of the Woman of Samaria is not about a woman preaching the Word. She told the Samaritans, *Come, and see a man, which told me all things that ever I did: is not this the Christ? Then they went out of the city, and came unto Him. John 4:29-30* She gave her testimony about a man who told her about her life and asked, is not this the Christ? She said, "Come see a man that told me everything I've ever done." Let's look at the words Jesus told her: "You are an adulteress and living with a man that is not your husband. In other words, He told her she was an adulteress. This does not sound like "go ye into all the world and preach the gospel."

If the Bible didn't say this, we should not say it either. Jesus did not commission her to preach, neither was she chosen by Him to preach. She shared her testimony much like we do when Christ does something for us. Also, Christ was still ministering and preaching, and He had not ascended. It wasn't His time. No one had been commissioned to go spread the Gospel of Jesus Christ at this time, because He was still present, teaching the disciples.

In the book of Judges the prophetess, Deborah is introduced. She judged Israel. Barak said unto her, if thou wilt go with me, then I will go but if thou wilt not go with me, then I will not go. As the story unfolded, she goes to battle with Barak (Kedesh), but Barak had the assignment not her. She was a prophetess. In the majority of scripture prophesies were delivered by men. This doesn't mean women didn't prophesy. The Lord's covenant people have been saved many times by spiritually in-tuned daughters of God. And though many women, including Rebekah, Hannah, Elisabeth, and Mary all prophesied, there are only a few who are designated as prophetess.

Other Matriarchs:

Miriam – the sister of Moses and Aaron. *Exodus 15:20, Micah 6:4* and *Exodus 15:20*

Deborah – The fourth judge in Israel. *Judges 5:7* and *Judges 4:4*

Huldah – Lived in the time of the righteous King Josiah. She prophesied that the wicked people of Judah would feel the wrath of God, but Josiah would be blessed. *Kings 22:14-20*

Isaiah's wife – Little is known of her, other than Isaiah calls her the prophetess.

Anna – Was an eighty-four-year-old widow who was present when Jesus was taken to the temple as a baby. Luke wrote that she departed not from the temple but served God with fastings and prayers night and day. *Luke 2:36-37*

Daughters of Philip – Philip, the Evangelist had four daughters, virgins, which prophesied. Acts 21:8-9

God used women throughout the Bible, but I have not found anywhere where God called a woman to preach, to the pastorate, an evangelist, apostle or bishop. There is no scriptural reference. Throughout my lifetime, I have been in court many times, as some know. Every time I was convicted there was always evidence. Whenever there is not enough evidence, the court would declare insufficient evidence and dismiss the case. God used men and women, but he used them differently. So, whenever you tell me something from the Bible, you should be able to go to the scripture and provide evidence. Where is the evidence that God told the woman to go into all the world and preach the gospel? Show me where He said that.

You never read in the scripture where a woman killed a lion or beat an army with the jawbone of a jackass. We never read where God told a woman to walk on the water. Where did God tell a woman that she would be the wisest woman to ever live? You never read anywhere in the Bible where God told the woman that through her seed the whole world would be blessed. You never read where God told any woman to go and tell Pharaoh to let my people go. It is plain where Jesus choose twelve disciples and told them to go into all the world. You never read anywhere, where Jesus told twelve women to go into all the world.

Again, I'm not saying He doesn't use women. I'm saying God uses people differently. He never said man was the weaker vessel. Why did He say that woman was the weaker vessel? As Christians when we say something to somebody, we should be able to show people by scripture exactly where we are coming from.

I Thessalonians 5:21 *Prove all things; hold fast that which is good.*

II Timothy 3:16 *All scripture is given by inspiration of God, and is profitable for doctrine, for reproof, for correction, for instruction in righteousness.*

Paul asserts the equality of the sexes: *There is neither Jew nor Greek, there is neither bond nor free, there is neither male nor female: for ye are all one in Christ Jesus.* **Galatians 3:28**

For church order and order of the family – **Ephesians 5:22-32**

Disorder, chaos and confusion – **I Corinthians 14:33**

Understanding God's order in both the family and the church causes us to realize that these limiting passages are not so much restrictive as protective. They protect women.

Paul writes to the church at Ephesus, *Wives, submit yourselves unto your own husbands, as unto the Lord. For the husband is the head of the wife, even as Christ is the head of the church: and he is the savior of the body. Therefore as the church is subject unto Christ, so let the wives be to their own husbands in everything. Husbands, love your wives, even as Christ also loved the church, and gave himself for it; That he might sanctify and cleanse it with the washing of water by the word. That he might present it to himself a glorious church, not having spot, or wrinkle, or any such thing; but that it should be holy and without blemish. So ought men to love their wives as their own bodies. He that loveth his wife loveth himself. For no man ever yet hated his own flesh: but nourisheth and cherisheth it, even as the Lord the church: For we are members of his body, of his flesh, and of his bones. For this cause shall a man leave his father and mother, and shall be joined unto his wife, and they two shall be one flesh. This is a great mystery: but I speak concerning Christ and the church Nevertheless let every one of you in particular so love his wife even as himself; and the wife see that she reverence her husband. Ephesians 5:32-33*

I say again, many equates their calling to preaching or being called into the pastorate, but there are many other callings. Let me also say that because you are a man in ministry doesn't mean you were called by God to preach, pastor a church, or become an evangelist, apostle or bishop. You can be successful doing the wrong thing, but God is not going to go against His Word. He is not going to tell a man that he is the head in their home and them allow a woman to usurp authority over him in the church. There is no question in my mind that God uses women, but in my study of God's Word, I recognize and believe that men and women are out of order.

I am in search of and studying the scriptures to discover the facts surrounding God using women in the same capacity as men, as it pertains to his church – the Body of Christ. My opinion and personal thoughts are irrelevant, the scripture alone bears proof. And anything that contradicts the scriptures is a liar! One woman told me, and I quote, "I know God uses me, and if He can use a jack-ass He can use me." I told this woman, "Well, God also used whales, frogs, doves, and other animals." Jesus referred to the rooster crowing, but He never told one of them to go preach. I just believe when we say things, we should base it upon the scripture alone.

I notice when people talk to me, many times they just speak out of their emotions. If you have evidence, go to the Bible and show me; book, chapter and verse. Show me where God commissioned a woman to preach, pastor, evangelize, or become an apostle or bishop. I have talked to preachers, pastors and bishops; to those in the pastorate, I have asked them the same question. Nobody. No preacher, bishop, Doctor, evangelist or pastor have shown me scriptures to support this fact. Mind you, I'm not saying that God can't use a woman. We have scriptures that prove God did use women. He used them differently. He used Deborah, the prophetess and judge of Israel to serve as a political and military leader during the period of the judges, when Israel had no king. Deborah wasn't the one that God called to go to battle, but she confirmed the word of God. She even went to battle with him, but the assignment was Barak's. *Judges 4:4-9* Deborah gave Barak a prophetic word, while operating in her calling as a prophetess.

Men are out of order and I make no excuses for the way women have been abused, mistreated, and placed in positions, which God never called them to. God is and will always be a God of order. I repeat this again because it is important that people know that God's Word stands true and never changes for anyone. My opinion doesn't matter but His Word does. God uses women throughout scripture, but He did not call women to lead the man or to usurp authority over the man. *Jesus saith unto her, Touch me not; for I am not yet ascended to My Father: but go to My brethren, and say unto them, I ascend unto my Father, and your Father: and to my God, and your God. Mary Magdalene came and told the disciples that she had seen the Lord, and that he had spoken these things unto her. John 20:17-18.*

I've heard many people say your sons and your daughters shall prophesy but prophesying and preaching are two different things.

Prophesy – means the inspired declaration of divine will and purpose. A prediction of something to come: A specified thing will happen in the future.

Preach – means to deliver a sermon or religious address to an assembled group of people, typically in church.

Testify – serve as evidence or proof of existence, or of being the case.

Testimony – a public recounting of a religious conversion or experience.

Usurp – take (a position of power or importance) illegally or by force. Take the place of (someone in a position of power) illegally; supplant.

Mary Magdalene was not commissioned to preach; she was instructed by God to go tell the brethren about his ascension unto His Father. That was it. It was not a sermon. He told her to tell the disciples what He had spoken to her. She did not preach, nor did she evangelize. She simply relayed a message. She hearkened to the voice of Jesus and obeyed what He said. Many people will mention the scripture in *Acts 2:17a. And it shall come to pass in the last days, saith God, I will pour out my Spirit on all flesh: and your sons and your daughters shall prophesy.* As we read this text, remember preaching and prophesy are two different gifts. They don't operate the same way, and you can't make God's word fit in a place somewhere it was not intended.

Joel 2:28 *And it shall come to pass afterward, that I will pour out my spirit upon all flesh; and your sons and your daughters shall prophesy, your old men shall dream dreams, your young men shall see visions:*

Prophesying is not preaching. Case in point: Noah for instance, God told Noah to tell the people it was going to rain, but this was a prophetic word. If God tells a woman or anybody to tell something, it's a prophetic word. Jonah was swallowed by a fish. God gave Jonah a prophetic word to tell the people to stop what they were doing. A prophetic word is when God gives you a message, a warning, to tell the people; good or bad. He used Nathan in *II Samuel 12* to rebuke David when he had taken Uriah, the Hittites wife. He also ordered Uriah to be killed. This was a prophetic word.

Preaching is exhibited in *Matthew 28:19: Go ye therefore, and teach all nations, baptizing them in the name of the Father, and of the Son, and of the Holy Ghost:* Preaching is carrying the Good News that Jesus Christ has come with a formula to save and change your life from sin. Acts 2 says, Then Peter said unto them, Repent, and be baptized every one of you in the name of Jesus Christ for the remission of sins, and ye shall receive the gift of the Holy Ghost. So, according to the gospel, preaching and prophesy are two different things. You can't intertwine the two; therefore, it needs to be understood that prophesy is not preaching.

Women have said, you mean to tell me that if I preach the Word of God, I'm going to die and go to hell? I tell them real quick that I did not say that, but let me tell you what the Word says: Many will come up in that day... (I don't want to be one of the many.) *Not everyone that saith unto me, Lord, Lord, shall enter into the kingdom of heaven; but he that doeth the will of my Father which is in heaven. Many will say to me in that day, Lord, Lord, have we not prophesied in thy name? and in thy name have cast out devils? and in thy name done many wonderful works? And then will I profess unto thee, I never knew you: depart from me, ye that work iniquity. Matthew 7:21-23*

This means that you can do many things in his name but here is the key; did he authorize you to use his name? Because when they came before Him and began to identify things they did in his name, he said, "I never knew you: depart from me, ye that work iniquity." Iniquity means to be against God. You can't use someone's name without them giving you the authority to use it. That's called forgery. And that's unlawful. If I were to do this today, I could be sentenced to jail. Remember the Bible says that this is a straight way. He said there would be few that find it. *Matthew 7:13,14.*

Again, there is no denying that women throughout the Bible were very strong, as there are still strong women today. But, I find no place as of yet where they are called to preach, be pastors, apostles, evangelist, elders or bishops. None usurped (*exercise*d) authority over the man. The first man, Adam was wrong from the beginning when he harkened to the voice of the woman instead of remaining obedient to the voice of God. I am not saying that man should not listen to the voice of his wife, but I am saying when God has spoken and said anything, we should his voice above all others. If you have scripture to support that God used women to Pastor or usurp authority over the man in the church, while not calling her to be head of the house, please show me? I want to know the truth.

I hear preachers telling lies from the pulpit and this hasn't always been so. Why would God change His order from the home to the church? He didn't do it. He set up the order of the home and the church. He does not contradict His Word.

Let me make it perfectly clear that I know many women who have served with me in the Body of Christ. I appreciate every woman who is steadfast, diligent, faithful and committed to God. I believe our country has done wrong, not supporting women and treating them unfairly in the workforce and in places of leadership. Women are a special gift from God to mankind. When God said, "it is not good that man should be alone," he made her as the helpmate suitable for man. The church has overstepped its boundaries in placing her in a role that God didn't call her to.

The church needs the love and nurturing that women bring to the home and to the church. God designed the relationship between man and woman to complement one another. He never intended them to be looked at in comparison, as one gender is better than the other. Our roles are different. We have rejected the God-given differences and it has led to an unbalanced view in the home and in the church. The role of man as leader is not a glorified position, but it is the role of a servant. A servant is called to protect, lead and guard the home and the church.

The position of men and pastors, in particularly, is to serve those God has entrusted in our care. This call is one of a servant-leader and protector. When we fail in our role as leaders and we give away our God-given headship, women step up and take over. When a woman takes over it's hard for men to regain their position as leaders and headship. Men must take a stand and be the men God has called, anointed and appointed. This authority has been bestowed on us and is not meant to be abusive or domineering. It is to be lived and exercised in humility and with gratitude. It's to be lived and demonstrated in love. *I Corinthians* 13 Pastors we are to serve those in church and not expect others to serve us. We are not to be lord over people, as if we are better than they. We should be approachable, not thinking of ourselves more highly than we ought to.

Men are given the positions of pastors and elders because God gave them the role of leading and dying for their family and the church. Remember, the way Christ lived is our example of how we should live. He led the people and He was a shepherd to all. Women and men are equal in Christ, but our roles, assignments and positions are different as it pertains to Christ and His Church. Jesus never disrespected women. He treated them with honor and respect, but he never reversed the role of men and women. He did not do it! Nowhere does the Bible support women pastors. I supported and licensed and ordained women, but I was wrong. I conformed to what others around me were doing. Again, if you are one of the women I licensed or ordained, I repent to you and to God because I cannot sanction or approve something he did not do.

Women can be queens, entrepreneurs, business professionals, judges, or hold any office outside the church. *Proverbs 31* exemplifies this type of woman: One who was resourceful, and the heart of her husband safely trusted her. She was the kind of wife any man would want, to bear his children and run his business. She, like many women, was very intelligent and trustworthy. This woman was submitted to God; so it was easy for her to submit to her husband. You have a lot of men who do not love their wives the way God commanded them.

If a man is a successful single male, he will most likely be a successful husband. You can decide like me, when I was drawn away of my own lust and enticed. Satan knew exactly what I liked; he knew what made me tingle. His objective was to get me away from God's assignment, because it was working mightily. I have learned that when God wants to bless you, He puts people in your life to support you. I've also learned when Satan wants to stop you, he also puts people in your life with the intent to distract you.

So, I hit this wall, and I've been working my way back ever since. I can't say that I haven't sinned or fallen short of the Word of God, because I have. I repented and asked God to restore me. I missed it. Much like many women and men of God today, we don't hearken to the voice of the Lord. He's always directing your path. If you are successful in life, it's your fault, and if you fail, it's your fault. Always remember you are the one writing this story.

Women need to stop asking men if they love them and start asking them where you are taking me? If a man is taking you somewhere, he must have a vision for (your) life. But some women do not have a submissive spirit to ask these questions. Some men have given women personal things that God gave them, and these women have stored them in their personal jewelry box. Men need to go and ask for their personal stuff back so they can be the man God called them to be. Amen!

GENDER ROLES IN MARRIAGE

Paul identifies the idea of "headship" for the husband, among other things.

Wives are instructed to submit to their husbands as to the Lord – *Wives, submit yourselves unto your own husbands, as unto the Lord. For the husband is the head of the wife, even as Christ is the head of the church: and he is the savior of the body. Therefore, as the church is subject unto Christ, so let the wives be to their own husbands in everything. Ephesians 5:22-24*

Husbands are identified as the "head" of the wife, as Christ is the head of the church – *For the husband is the head of the wife, even as Christ is the head of the church: and he is the savior of the body. Ephesians 5:23*

Husbands are instructed to love their wives sacrificially, as Christ loved the Church, and as their own bodies – *Husbands, love your wives, even as Christ also loved the church, and gave himself for it; That he might sanctify and cleanse it with the washing of water by the word, That he might present it to himself a glorious church, not having spot, or wrinkle, or any such thing; but that it should be holy and without blemish. So, ought men to love their wives as their own bodies. He that loveth his wife loveth himself. For no man ever yet hated his own flesh; but nourisheth and cherisheth it, even as the Lord the church: Ephesians 5:25-29*

You romance her before marriage and believed to have fallen in love with her. You may still be disconnected from her. I went to a restaurant and there was a couple there. I watched them as they sat together but were glued to their cell phones. I went to the man and told him, "Man, you need to put that phone down and enjoy your wife." The first thing he did was to blame his wife and say, "She's on hers too." I told him, "But you are the man." I didn't know this couple, but the Holy Spirit directed me to speak into their lives. It's not that the Holy Spirit does not lead, but we must be submitted and in tuned to Him. I have done the same thing countless times in restaurants, Wal-Mart, or wherever. If God tells me to say something, I say it.

Wives are instructed to give respect to their husbands – *Nevertheless let every one of you in particular so love his wife even as himself; and the wife see that she reverences her husband. Ephesians 5:33*

Man is described as the glory of God, and woman is described as the glory of man – *For a man indeed ought not to cover his head, forasmuch as he is the image and glory of God: but the woman is the glory of the man. For the mans is not of the woman; but the woman of the man. Neither was the man created for the woman; but the woman for the man. I Corinthians 11:7-9*

Both man and woman should be saved and submitted to God and to one another. *Ephesians 5:21* Men, God has not called you to follow the woman but to love her as He loved the church, giving his life for it. He called you to be the head of the woman. God is very gender oriented. It is obvious that there is a significant difference between men and women. It's also important to note that differing roles does not indicate differing value or intelligence or honor. Yet, God did create us with gender roles, so it behooves us to seek and understand His choice.

Understanding each example and learning more about their meaning:

- Adam was placed with an assignment first
- God planted the garden for Adam and brought Adam to the garden. Genesis 2:8
- Adam was given work to do prior to being given a wife. We have no record of Eve specifically being given work. Genesis 2:15
- God commands Adam not to eat of the forbidden fruit. We don't find anywhere God instructed the woman not to eat of the forbidden fruit. I strongly believe that Adam gave instructions to Eve as God gave them to him. He was operating in leadership before the Lord gave him a helpmate. Genesis 2:16-17
- Eve, his wife was created as a suitable helper; a helpmate to fit in and to adapt to the assignment God gave Adam, not Eve. Genesis 2:18
- Adam named the animals, not Eve. Genesis 2:20
- Eve was created from the man, not Adam from Eve. Genesis 2:21-22
- Eve was brought to the man, not the Man to Eve. Genesis 2:22
- Both Adam and Eve were created in the image of God Genesis 1:26-28

- Adam and Eve were commanded to be fruitful and multiply Genesis 1:28
- Adam was created outside the garden from the dust of the ground, while Eve was created inside the garden from a part of Adam. Genesis 2

NEITHER MALE NOR FEMALE

Many women and men refer to the scripture by saying God put no difference between male or female. This is said in order to indicate that God does not see gender when it comes to the role of a woman in ministry. This is not what Paul was saying at all. *Galatians 3:28 states: There is neither Jew nor Greek, there is neither bond nor free, there is neither male nor female: for ye are all one in Christ Jesus.* This points out, there is neither Jew nor Greek, slave or free, male or female. Some suggests that all gender roles are, in Christ, rendered out of date because of this; however, it was Paul who wrote this, and he is the one who comes under fire the most for making gender distinctions in his writing.

This scripture refers to our standing in salvation: Jewish believers have no better place before God than Gentile believers, and men have no greater standing in salvation than women. So, the Bible does tend to reveal a distinction in roles. Men were created first and given work to do, and the woman was given to the man in marriage. Women seem to have been specifically created for relationship, and in marriage, are specifically instructed to be submissive to the headship of the man. Man is responsible to treat the woman with sacrificial love. Again, I say, women can be queens, entrepreneurs, business professional, judges, or hold any office outside the church. Proverbs 31 displays the woman in business.

I submit again the problem falls on man. We listen to

people and not God, and this has gotten us in trouble. *Now the Spirit speaketh expressly, that in the latter times some shall depart from the faith, giving heed to seducing spirits, and doctrines of devils; Speaking lies in hypocrisy; having their conscience seared with a hot iron; I Timothy 4:1-2.* God is telling us that we are out of order. We're disconnected and don't know it! In Matthew 24:10-12, 24 Christ speaks about how there would be many false prophets arising and we currently have many false prophets among us today. Search the scriptures for yourself. If I'm wrong concerning the call of women by God, show me scriptures supporting your findings. If I'm wrong, I'll say I'm wrong. But if I'm correct and you can't find scripture to support what you're promoting in your churches, then you need to turn in your ordination certificates and licenses and stop saying God called you to usurp authority over men.

Pastors, you need to stop placing women in roles that God has not sanctioned or ordained. The reason our homes, communities, churches, and government are out of order is because God gave man dominion. God put man in place first. I know He gave man and woman dominion; I understand that man controls the thermostat. Marriages, families, communities, and government are doing things contrary to the Word of God because men are controlling the thermostat. When God came into the Garden of Eden, He looked for the person that controlled the thermostat – Adam. But Adam gave the thermostat to Eve, and the next thing we learn is Adam and Eve were living among the bushes. He gave his authority to the woman to control the thermostat like many husbands do in their homes. Many pastors have done the same in the church. *We Are Disconnected and Don't Know It!*

THE POSITION OF THE MAN
THE POSITION OF THE WOMAN
I TIMOTHY 3:1-16

Paul starts this chapter by saying that if a *man*, not a woman, desires the office of a bishop, *he* desires a good work. A bishop then must be blameless, the *husband* of one wife, not the wife of one husband. *One that ruleth well his own house, having his children in subjection with all gravity; (For if the man knows not how to rule his own house, how shall he take care of the church of God?) I Timothy 3:4-5 The husband is the head of the wife, even as Christ is the head of the church: and he is the savior of the body. Therefore, as the church is subject unto Christ, so let the wives be to their own husbands in everything. Ephesians 5:23-24* I didn't say this Paul did; if a *man* knows not how to *rule his* own house, how shall *he* take care of the church of God?

The scripture does not say if a *woman* knows not how to rule *her own* house... God did not call the woman to rule in the home nor in the church. The question asked how shall *he* the man take care of the church of God? God did not call woman to take care of His church; he didn't call a man to take care of the church if he is not being the man of his household. Instead, he is being a weak kneed, jelly back man listening to the voice of his wife, not listening or obeying the voice of God. At home he is Reverend Honey Do. Honey do whatever I say, and that is what honey does.

In church he chastises, rebukes and puts everyone in their place. A simple look from his wife and he knows how to respond. Next, he changes his sermons, and the cycle never ends.

God called man to take care of his church but he never gave man the authority to put his wife or any other woman in the position of pastor, bishop, apostle or evangelist. Again, I say, "we" men have bestowed positions on one another: Reverend, Doctor, Bishop, First Lady and etcetera. The scriptures say, *because it is written, be ye holy; for I am holy. I Peter 1:16* Throughout this chapter the writer refers to the male role, and we cannot add or take away from the scriptures. I *Thessalonians 5:21* states, *prove all things; hold fast that which is good.* Timothy writes, *all scripture is given by inspiration of God, and is profitable for doctrine, for reproof, for correction, for instruction in righteousness: II Timothy 3:16* Some have said that Paul was a feminist, but the scripture says, all scripture is given by inspiration of God. God does not contradict Himself.

II Peter 1:20-21 *Knowing this first, that no prophecy of the scripture is of any private interpretation.*

For the prophecy came not in old time by the will of man: but holy men of God spake as they were moved by the Holy Ghost.

Why would God place man as head in his home, but then put woman in the church to usurp authority over the man? I ask you brothers and sisters as you read this information, please don't read anything into what I haven't said. I am earnestly seeking the truth of God's Holy Scriptures. From my studies of the scriptures I haven't found where God called women to pastor, be bishops, evangelist or apostles. If this is true, then I too have erred in the past and I can no longer lead anyone astray because I have adhered to man and not God. To the women whom I have pastored, licensed and ordained, I was wrong. I have not found anywhere in the scriptures where God supports women leading the man in the church. To those I have led wrong; their blood is on my hand. For this reason, I send this letter to you.

I cannot find one scripture where God called women to be apostles, pastors, bishops, evangelists or preachers. I have diligently searched the scriptures and I welcome anyone to show me where God called women to any of these roles. The scriptures provide sufficient proof that God called men to each of these roles. As Christians, we should be able to identify the scriptures that give reasons for what we believe. If I can't, then I'm wrong. You can't make wrong right when no one wants to say anything. We wonder why the church is the way it is today. The Bible said the love of many would wax cold.

When it comes to preaching you should be very careful how you let people treat you, and I learned this when I was in the pastorate. The reason preachers put a lot of women in leadership is because women are great fundraisers. Because they raise money well, pastors allow them to lead. They don't want to shut them up. They know when it's anniversary time, Sister So-and-so will look out for the

Pastor. I learned this when I was a Pastor. You must be very careful how you let people treat you and what you let people do for you. Every dime that comes to you should not be taken because some people don't have the best intentions. Don't do it. If Jesus had concerns about what people called him, so should you. Do you remember the story when the man came to Jesus and called him Good Master? Jesus asked him why he called him good. *Luke 18:19*

You can't let anyone call you something Jesus did not call you. It is one thing for them to call you Holy Brother - that's alright, but how many times do you hear that? We are more concerned with titles such as bishops. Some say, "You know I'm a bishop now or you know I'm a preacher now? I'm a Pastor, or I'm an apostle now." We are more concerned about these titles more than their functions. The title does not make things happen. It's the function of the title. We wear the title like we are somebody great! The Bible tell us in *Ephesians 4:12* that the gifts are for the perfecting of the saints. So, if you say you are a bishop, apostle, pastor or evangelist, how are you perfecting God's people? They don't belong to you, they are God's people, and he told you to make disciples of them. You are making church members of them instead, because if you were making disciples the streets would not be as they are today. Today, people go to church and then to the nearest Golden Corral in order to get anything they want from the buffet bar.

Matthew 7:21-24 *Not everyone that saith unto me, Lord, Lord, shall enter into the kingdom of heaven; but he that doeth the will of my Father which is in heaven.*

Many will say to me in that day, Lord, Lord, have we not prophesied in thy name? And in thy name have cast out devils? And in thy name done many wonderful works?

And then will I profess unto them, I never knew you: depart from me, ye that work iniquity.

Therefore whosoever heareth these sayings of mine, and doeth them, I will liken him unto a wise man, which built his house upon a rock:

Christ has not given us authority over many of the things we allow and even teach in church. These things makes us frauds, and we continue to sign His name and endorse them as things he commissioned us to do. I have biblically supported my statements, and these are not my words, they are the Word of God — written by men who were moved by the Spirit of God and this is not forgery. If God did not give you authority to use His name, then you are wrong. You are committing a criminal act by signing his name to things that he did not give you. If God put a woman over a man then that makes God a liar. The Bible says, *God is not a man, that He should lie; neither the son of man, that he should repent: hath he said, and shall he not do it? Or hath he spoken, and shall he not make it good? Numbers 23:19*

Pastor – a minister in charge of a church or congregation.

Preacher – A person who preaches, especially a minister of religion. To preach, deliver a sermon or religious address to an assembled group of people, typically in church. Publicly proclaim or teach (a religious message or belief.)

Evangelist – A person who seeks to convert others to the Christian faith, especially by public preaching.

Prophet – A person regarded as an inspired teacher or proclaimer of the will of God. A person who advocates or speaks in a visionary way about a new belief, cause or theory.

Prophetess – A female prophet.

Apostle – The twelve chief disciples of Jesus Christ. A vigorous and pioneering advocate or supporter of particular policies, ideas or causes.

Bishop – a senior member of the Christian clergy, typically in charge of a diocese empowered to confer holy orders.

The actions of a believer should be predicated upon the Word of God. If we base our lives on Biblical instructions, then we should live accordingly. If we are not going to do what the Bible says, then we should just toss the Bible away and do things the way we want. Any time you say you are called or commissioned to do something for God you should be able to support it through scripture.

Titus 2: 3-5 - *The aged women likewise, that they be in behavior as becometh holiness, not false accusers, not given to much wine, teachers of good things; That they may teach* *the young women to be sober, to love their husbands, to love their children, to be discreet, chaste, keepers at home, good, obedient to their own husbands, that the word of God be not blasphemed.*

God is a God of order; and God does use women, but not in the same capacity as men. God does not set up the family one way and then changes his order when it comes to His church. God was very selective in His calling. In Matthew 10:1-5 we read where Jesus called His disciples. When the scripture says he called *them*, it means there were more than twelve that were present, and from them he was very selective in the men he picked. Many times, during Jesus' ministry men, women, children and disciples were present. The disciples were followers of Christ. During this particular occasion he chose twelve men (each of them were named.) All were men, and he commissioned them according to his will.

During another occasion He picked seventy and all of them were men. *Luke 10:1* state, *after these things the Lord appointed other seventy also, and sent them two and two before his face into every city and place, whither he himself would come.* In *Luke 6:13-15* we observe Jesus calling his disciples, and from those gathered he chose twelve whom he named apostles. This again demonstrates him as very selective. He called the twelve by name, and they were all men. The twelve tribes of Israel were all men. He called Noah to build the ark. He called Abraham to go to a land that He would show him. He commissioned

Moses to go before the Pharaoh when the cries of His people came before Him. One story after another demonstrates God's calling, selection, and anointing of men to lead His people.

He put the man out front; not the woman. Again, I'm not saying that God does not use women because we read where he did, but as it pertains to the position of order – he used men. The scripture provides a pattern of God's order. In the case of God's church, he never called a woman as a first lady, co-pastor, deaconess, evangelist or elder. Men and church organizations have done this. I believe men and women are out of order. How can you be a Christian and not do what the Bible says? People get in trouble because they do not follow the pattern of God – drawn away by their own lust and enticed. An example of co-pastor can be seen with Moses as he went away to meet with God. He left Aaron in charge and he messed up the church. He was disconnected and didn't even know it. Aaron listened to the people and it got him and them in trouble.

You can't have two leaders at the same time. God only talks to the leader. When God spoke to Saul, he disobeyed God. He did something different than what God told him. (He called himself helping God.) But God does not need help and like Saul, man has changed what God has stated in his Word. We now have a homosexual Bible. God gave men the authority to walk in His Word, but many have walked away and given themselves to everyone else but God. God only honors His word. We should not live one way at home and another way at church. God's word has been given to us to follow. Read the story in II Kings 5 about Naaman. Naaman offered the man of God presents when he was healed of leprosy, but the man of God refused it. He states: *As the Lord liveth, before whom I stand, I will receive none. II Kings 5:16a* In other words, the prophet was saying that it was God who performed the miracle and he could not charge payment for God's work.

Naaman responded with understanding, but referred to the prophets' servant, Gehazi, who travelled with him. He had a different motive than Elisha. He saw all that money going down the road and he went behind the man of God's back and lied to Naaman. He told Naaman that the prophet changed his mind. He took items home and privately hid them in his house, but his actions placed his entire family in jeopardy. Many preachers are doing the same thing today because they refuse to stand up for what is right. They are getting their entire family in trouble because of greed. You think you're blessed because you have a lot of material things? When you are not in the will of God you are actually operating under a curse. I don't care who you are or who you think you are. This is why the Bible says, *For what shall it profit a man, if he shall gain the whole world, and lose his own soul? Mark 8:36* You can't stop there because it goes further to ask the following: *Or what shall a man give in exchange for his soul? Mark 8:37* This man lost his entire family because of greed. Greed is a hell of thing... and I'm not cursing because hell is in the Bible. When he returned before his master Elisha, he was asked where he had been. Gehazi lied again, and the leprosy that had plagued Naaman was now on him and his seed forever. Greed is a hell of a thing.

If ninety-nine percent of what you do is within the interior of your church it's a good indicator that God didn't call you. Countless churches are having revival but doing the work of the church eliminates the need to have revival. You may need encouragement or motivation to continue things, but revival means you are about dead. Every year some churches have two or three revivals and their actions say they are dying three or four times a year. "Time for another revival," they say. "We're about dead" A good example is someone in a swimming pool who goes under the water about three of four times. You jump into the pool and pull them out. They perhaps came near the point of death – unable to breathe because their lungs are filled with water. To revive them, you have to pump that water out of their lungs in order to restore life and they are able to breathe again. But for the believer who have the Holy Ghost, how can you revive the Holy Ghost? You may need encouragement or exhortation in righteousness, but revival? You are saved; you are the righteousness of God. It does not make sense.

We use words in the church that are not right. You cannot revive Holy Ghost filled people. Jesus is the answer to the world's need. So, when he came, he said he would reprove the world of sin, and of righteousness, and of judgment *John 16:8* He came to seek and save those which were lost. *(Matthew 18:11)* I can understand seeking inspirational or a week of encouragement, because I know we go through things: trials and tribulations, and the Bible says we should encourage one another. Paul told Peter there would come a time when men would not endure sound doctrine. *(II Timothy 4:3)* Timothy was reminded of his unfeigned (genuine, sincere) faith that was in his grandmother Lois and his mother Eunice and was encouraged that the same faith was in him.

The warning was given that perilous times would come, but Timothy was told to be instant in season; out of season. Men must stand up. Just like Adam in the Garden of Eden, men see things but refuse to say anything. You can't believe in half truths. If someone asks you something and you can't show them within the scriptures, then you are simply telling people what you think or giving your opinion only. But it is not the Word of God. I do not intend to hurt your feelings, but these are your thoughts and philosophies. People get mad when you tell them the truth, and I've seen people get angry when you tell them what the Bible says.

God does refer to gender. You've never seen a woman fight a giant. But David did. So, where did God use a woman to push the pillars of a building down? He didn't. He used Samson. Man is the protector of the woman. In the case of a home invasion, a woman doesn't tell her husband, "Honey you just lay here. I'm going to go take care of this." We have a lot of weak, jelly-backed men that refuse to stand up and be men. Man has turned the church into a mom and pop business. Everyone in your family has a position and that makes it no longer God's house, but your house. However, when trouble breaks you say you're not going to take over God's house, but as soon as things settle, you're back to you and your family church. Again, if the word of God is silent, we should be silent. There was a time when the church was different. We've brought the world into the church; line dancing and prosperity pushing rather than preaching the gospel of Jesus Christ.

People are skilled with speaking but know very little about the scriptures and equate the skill of speaking with the calling to preach. Women are teaching males how to be good men, and too many are without their fathers. I know cases where mothers have problems with their daughters and are forced to send them to their fathers for discipline and stern rearing. We need these strong father-figures in the lives of our children. There are going to be many people in that day that say Lord, Lord, and God is going to tell them I never knew you. Pastors with three members call themselves Bishops. Then, his wife gets pregnant and he becomes an apostle. Many men call themselves apostles now, but an apostle is one that makes sure the church is governed by the Word of God. Apostles keep the church in line with God's word.

Jesus was master and teacher, but Jesus did not tell people to call him a title. Titles do not make you. Another reason churches have revivals is because they are not doing what they're supposed to do. And why call ye me, Lord, Lord, and do not the things which I say? Luke 6:46 Please do not tell me how you feel, think, or what your theory is. I don't care. Christians have a responsibility to solely speak based on the Word of God. Quote the scriptures only, and do not add or take away.

There is a difference between ministering and preaching. In *Acts 18:26*, Pricilla and Aquila did not preach. She and her husband expounded and explained the scripture. *And it shall come to pass in the last days, saith God, I will pour out of my Spirit upon all flesh: and your sons and your daughters shall prophesy, and your young men shall see visions, and your old men shall dream dreams. Acts 2:17* To understand where the good and the evil come from, we must understand the law and order of God. *Genesis 1:14* says, *And God said, Let there be lights in the firmament of the heaven to divide the day from the night; and let them be for signs, and for seasons, and for days, and years:* This was God's law and order, and when we move contrary to this we move away from God, and we see the first account of this with the war in heaven. *Isaiah 14:12*

WAR IN HEAVEN – THE GARDEN OF EDEN

If Satan could cause commotion in heaven and get a third of the angels to rebel against God, what do you think he can do here on earth? *Revelation 12:7-12 says, And there was war in heaven: Michael and his angels fought against the dragon; and the dragon fought and his angels, And prevailed not; neither was their place found any more in heaven. And the great dragon was cast out, that old serpent, called the Devil, and Satan, which deceiveth the whole world: he was cast out into the earth, and his angels were cast out with him. And I heard a loud voice saying in heaven, Now is come salvation, and strength, and the kingdom of our God, and the power of his Christ: for the accuser of our brethren is cast down, which accused them before our God day and night. And they overcame him by the blood of the Lamb, and by the word of their testimony; and they loved not their lives unto death. Therefore rejoice, ye heavens, and ye that dwell in them. Woe to the inhibiters of the earth and of the sea! For the devil is come down unto you, having great wrath, because he knoweth that he hath but a short time.*

Ezekiel 28:14-15 *Thou art the anointed cherub that covereth; and I have set thee so: thou wast upon the holy mountain of God; thou hast walked up and down in the midst of the stones of fire.*

Thou wast perfect in thy ways from the day that thou wast created, till iniquity was found in thee.

Satan is on a mission to get back at God. Everything he does is opposite of God. He is not a man but a spirit that works in man. In the book of Ezekiel, the Lord talks about the angel he made. This angel is Lucifer: Devil and Satan are other titles, but Lucifer is a name. Lucifer was God's creation, and has been documented among other prominent angels, including Michael, Gabriel and Raphael. Lucifer was not always a devil. In *Ezekiel 28:13* the scripture describes Lucifer, the angel, and not the devil. Snake or serpent is another title associated with the devil. The tongue of the serpent has a split at its tip, symbolizing confusion, and Satan will disguise himself to convince the believer he's right. The devil is a deceiver; arrogant, prideful, self-willed, and has a hatred for God. His mission is to get back at God, and he uses mankind to achieve this.

Let me remind you the way a serpent works: When he wants to destroy something or someone he starts at the head. *II Corinthians 10:4-5* says, *(For the weapons of our warfare are not carnal, but mighty through God to the pulling down of strong holds:) Casting down imaginations, and every high thing that exalteth itself against the knowledge of God, and bringing into captivity every thought to the obedience of Christ;* Additionally, *I Corinthians 11:3* reads, *But I would have you know, that the head of every man is Christ; and the head of the woman is the man; and the head of Christ is God.* And this is why Satan comes to make war with our intellect and mind. He comes at our mind first. In the church, he attacks leadership, and in the home, his target is the man. Both are the headships.

Satan studies his prey, and one thing about the serpent, he is a master of patience. When the book says, "that old serpent," it refers to acknowledging the nature of the snake. A snake coils itself around its prey and suffocates it victim. When the prey is dead the snake begins the process of digestion. First, he attacks the head, then coils himself around each connection, and through the things of the world suffocates God out of the lives of churches and homes. This is done to rob people and places of spiritual wellness. When you feel yourself wanting to rearrange the vision or plans God has given the pastor, because you have a better one, it is the spirit of the devil at work. When you're feeling like you do not have to listen to your pastor anymore, because you have more education, the spirit of the devil is present. And when you find yourself getting up and walking out of the service, because in yourself righteous thinking you think you can do things better, the spirit of the devil has influenced.

Although, people are getting saved, delivered and set free, and the gospel is being preached to the poor, you become a whisperer in the church with the objective of being divisive toward the Pastor, the spirit of the devil has taken control. The Pastor asks if God has shown you anything and you say, "No." He tells you, well God has shown me. And he tells you what God showed him, and the church witnessed it come to pass. You try to bring in a worldly system when

God told his people to walk by faith and not by sight, that's the spirit of the devil. The motivations behind most power take-overs are jealousy and hatred: The desire to make one's name great. This was Satan's motivation when he said *"I will ascend into heaven, I will exalt my throne above the stars of God:" Isaiah 14:13b*

Satan's self-centeredness manifests as a spirit of selfishness: Everything was about "I". He was determined to destroy God and take God's place. It is a common saying that misery loves company. And if misery loves company, you get a person who hates the truth, they got the preaching itch, and do not want to follow leadership. In their mind, God talks to them almost 24 hours a day. This person goes throughout the congregation to manipulate those who are already weak and spiritually vulnerable and befriends them. This person is incompetent on their own, so they try to build off what is built or being built. The devil manifests as the spirit of jealousy, arrogance, hatred, competition, and high mindedness. He puts these traits in man as well. When you begin to feel like you want to take over things, and you are not the pastor, that is the spirit of Satan.

Now the devil is foolishly bold. This spirit wanted to replace God, which was an act of disrespect. He got tired of God being God, and iniquity was found in him. He did not simply leave. When a person becomes envious, hateful, spiteful, and despises authority, they begin spreading their hatred among others. The devil doesn't want you to know or be aware of his action. The scripture says don't be ignorant of Satan's devices. *II Corinthians 2:11* In order to avoid ignorance, preachers must tell the congregant about Satan and his devices. *Ezekiel 28* speaks about the multitude of his merchandise. He has wickedness in him, and his objective is to turn the children of God against one another. Leaders must tell the people of God the truth of God's Word.

When God created the earth, he put Adam and Eve in charge. I want to remind you that Satan tried to reverse the divine role of God in heaven, and he tried to do the same thing in the Garden of Eden. Satan did not get Adam with the fruit it was Eve. She was his distraction; she started looking at the tree while Satan talked to her. He convinced her to take the fruit. Then, she ate it and handed it to her husband. One of the worse things Adam did was listening to her without saying anything. He could have said something, but he kept silent and ate the fruit. Adam was placed with the first assignment; God gave him dominion. I submit unto you that He gave him total dominion and never took it back even unto this day!

Today, men are still trying to correct Adam's mistake in the garden. This is a Kingdom problem. God gave Adam total authority to name the animals and care for the Garden. God put Adam in place first. Then God said it was not good for Adam to be alone. So, God made a helpmate suitable for Adam: adaptable, to fit in. The Bible says that they were one flesh. This means they were in a different relationship. First, Adam was in a relationship with God, but when the woman was given to him, the relationship was altered and made different. I hear preachers today say when God called them, he called their wife too. Remember, God made Eve a helpmate. I have never read where God called Eve to help name the animals.

First, God said I'm going to make Adam, a helpmate to fit in and adapt to wherever he needed. I never read where God called her to name the animals. This is because Adam had already been given the assignment; Adam was focused on his assignment. This is not a put down, but women are very emotional. For many women it's hard for them to go through the mall and not touch something: a dress, pair of shoes, scarf, or handbag. These are things that are pleasant to her eyes, the same way the tree was to Eve in the garden. Many times, women spend money they don't even have because of how something looks. There's nothing wrong with her as an emotional being, but do not let your emotions pull you from the assignment of God. Eve had an assignment. Her assignment was to keep Adam company. *And the Lord God said, It is not good that the man should be alone; I will make him a help meet for him. Genesis 2:18* And we read further, *But for Adam there was not found a help meet for him. And the Lord God caused a deep sleep to fall upon Adam, and he slept: and he took one of his ribs, and closed up the flesh instead thereof; And the rib, which the Lord God had taken from man, made he a woman, and brought her unto the man. And Adam said, This is now bone of my bones, and flesh of my flesh: she shall be called Woman, because she was taken out of Man. Genesis 2:20b-23*

God commanded Adam not to eat of the forbidden

fruit. We do not read where God instructed the woman from eating. I strongly believe that Adam gave instructions to Eve as God gave them to him. He was operating in leadership before the Lord gave him a helpmate. *Genesis 2:16-17* It was Adams responsibility to tell Eve. Eve erroneously did four things; she looked at the tree, she took from the tree, she ate of the tree, and she gave to her husband the fruit of the tree. (I am mad at Adam today.) He did not have to eat of the fruit. Just like many preachers today, they refuse to say anything when their wives tell them things God should be telling them. Stuff like, "God told us to build a church." I've experienced this myself. My wife wanted to know where she was going to sit in the pulpit. I am glad my friend, Bishop Wright, heard me tell her that I wasn't going to get in trouble with God. I told her she would sit in the pews with everybody else.

Remember, Satan's objective has been to reverse the leadership roles. He tried to do it in heaven he couldn't get Adam, but he was successful with Eve. Instead of Eve going to her husband and saying, "Baby the serpent is talking to me," she took ownership of herself and was drawn away by her own lust and enticed. She ate the fruit, and gave to her husband, and he did eat as well. God punished the serpent and Eve, and when he spoke with Adam, the first thing God said because you listened to your wife and not me...Then he punished Adam. This happens to many ministers today: Instead of listening to God, they listen to their wives. The Bible tells us, *If any man come to me, and hate not his father, and mother, and wife, and children, and brethren, and sisters, yea, and his own life also, he cannot be my disciple. Luke 14:26* As God told Adam, he tells us the same. God still holds man responsible today. He called man to be the head and the leader, not the woman.

ROLE REVERSAL

One of the greatest tragedies to the black community was when slaves were brought to America and given reversed roles. The black man was taken out of position and was replaced by the woman. Willie Lynch, a British slave owner in the West Indies, allegedly wrote to the Colony of Virginia in 1712. Bear in mind that Satan's first attack is in the mind. This is what Willie Lynch did. His thoughts were, if I can get their mind, I can control everything.

As I began to talk about Role Reversal, let me thank God for all my white brothers and sisters in the Lord. Let me explain, from a black perspective, how this has affected us. This is Satan's strategy to destroy the black family – to mess us up and get us out of order. We have failed in recognizing that Satan is a strategist. From the time he was kicked out of heaven into the earth realm, his scheme has been to interrupt the plan of God for mankind. To help you to understand, let me take you back to slavery. To a time and place where a man named Willie Lynch implemented a strategy to show slave owners how to destroy and divide the black family. He published a plan to take the black man, woman and their children out of place.

The Bible states a house divided cannot stand. *Matthew 12:25* and *Mark 3:25* I read the Willie Lynch letter and saw how his strategy worked. I believe there are many blacks who survived slavery and got free from this mentality and way of thinking. But there are many who are still connected to this philosophy today and don't know it. They are disconnected and don't even know they are disconnected. This letter was allegedly written in the 1800's by a man named Willie Lynch. I apologize in advance for the language in the letter, but in order for you to get the true effects, you must hear it in the language it was written. As you read this letter, some things I assume will hurt, but the Bible declares that you shall know the truth and the truth will make you free. John 8:32 We must understand why we are like we are today. Again, I apologize for the language which will be offensive.

This message is said to have been presented on the bank of the James River, where Willie Lynch was invited to the colony of Virginia in 1712 to teach his own method of training slaves and slave owners. He promoted that if they used his methods it would last for three hundred or more years and after that the slaves would become distrustful of one another. Some of his methods of controls were inducing fear, distrust and envy for the purpose of control. He also used age, sex, intelligence, size of plantation, status on the plantation, and the attitude of the owners. Also, the use of the location of the slaves against them; texture of hair: fine or course; and their statue: tall or short to cause friction among themselves. He assured them that teaching distrust was stronger than trust, and envy was stronger than respect or appreciation. He assured them that the black slaves, after being treated this way consistently, would become self-refueling for hundreds and maybe even thousands of years to come.

He instructed them to make sure they put the old black male against the young male and the dark skinned against the light ones. Pit the female against the male and the male against the female. And above all, know how necessary it is that the slaves trust and depend on their masters, the white man. Slaves had to be treated in such a way that they loved, respected, and trusted their owners only. If they did these things, they would have control over their slaves for years to come. If used consistently for one year, the slaves themselves will remain unendingly distrustful of each other.

His method was to study human nature, and then the nature of slaves. His thoughts, if true, would break man and make a slave. "Take a black nigger boy and a pregnant nigger woman and her baby nigger boy. Second, you use the same method you would use in breaking a horse. We take the horse and break them from one form of life to another. We reduce them from their wild state or their natural state and cause them to become dependent on their owner, and then we can use them for our own self pleasure or business." His method was to keep the body of the slave while taking full control of the mind, thereby breaking the will to resist the slave owner. He further aimed to break the female mother, influencing her to pass the same mentality on to her children.

When her offspring were old enough to work, mothers would give them to the slave owner because her will was broken. She was trained to watch slave owners destroy the dignity and will of the male slave. This was done by stripping him of his clothes in front of the other male and female slaves, old and young alike and whip him to the point of death. Owners wanted slaves to be fearful but not dead, in order for the strong black nigger to be used for breeding and production. As women were made to become psychologically independent, they trained their daughters to be the same. This created the nigger woman out front while placing the nigger man following behind her and petrified.

Beforehand, slave owners were afraid to sleep at night for fear of being killed by their slaves. But after implementing Lynch's method, owners sleep soundly knowing that slave women stood guard. By the time the nigger boy was a young teen, he was broken and ready for long-term use and skillful work. He produced great labor use and destroyed the protective male image among slaves. This approach created a passive and dependent mindset within the nigger male slave and broke their will to resist. The breaking process was used for both horse and the nigger. They were to always be mindful of the female and offspring. Slavery promoted money and power; it made for sound economics. The slave owners were not to focus on the generation of the first broken slaves, but rather, future generations. If they broke the female mother, she would in turn break the offspring in the early stages of growth. When the child is of age to work the nigger, the mother would bring the child to the slave owner. Her normal, female, protecting tendencies would be broken. Her will would be diminished, reducing her to eating out of slave owner's hands and teaching her offspring to do the same.

Breaking the uncivilized nigger was done using the same method, varying in degree and level. The pressure had to be stepped up to complete a reversal of the mind. The meanest and most agitated nigger had to be stripped naked in front of all the other niggers, tar and feather him while his legs are tied to a different horse as they are faced in opposite directions, set him on fire, and beat the horses so they pull him apart as the other niggers watched. Then, take a bull whip and beat the other nigger males to the point of death in front of the females and the children, stopping short of killing him to put the fear of God in him and others. Then, use him for future reproduction.

Speaking from the black experience, I have witnessed this systematic infiltration in our society today among blacks and whites; males and females, and this plan has adversely affected the black community. In 2016, more than 40.2 million blacks lived in the US, and in 2017 more than 475,900 blacks were incarcerated in either state or federal prison. Blacks make up only 12% of the population in the U.S., but they represent 33% of the prison population. Conversely, of the 233.7 million whites in the US, 436, 500 are imprisoned. Whites represent 64% of population in the U.S., and 30% of the prison population. The Bible speaks of Satan as a serpent, and anytime a serpent gets ready to devour something he starts at the head. That is what has happened in the black community. Many of our old and young black men are unfortunately out of place.

Satan has in essence infiltrated our society with a welfare system. When Moses was bringing the children of Israel out of Egypt, they were living off a welfare system. The people didn't have to worry about food because God fed them daily. Their clothes didn't wear out, neither did their shoes wear away. They had a universal medical plan, where no one got sick. But when Joshua took over, they went from welfare to warfare. They had to march around the wall of Jericho. The Bible says they marched seven days, but on the seventh day they marched seven times: They blew the trumpets and let out a shout and the wall fell down flat. *Joshua 6:20*

A mother of two or three children could get welfare as long as the male was not in the home. Blacks were the ones who came up with the equal rights movement, but it turns out this movement over time presented and protected other movements that are against the Word of God. Now remember these were some very graphic details but we are experiencing many of these occasions today. Whites ask why we still talk about slavery. We talk about it because it is still at work. The black man's value is reduced to a price set forth by the white man. Blacks are viewed as three-fifths of a person for the purposes of taxation and representation after the new constitution acknowledged the institution of slavery. Slave owners looked for ways to make their slaves completely dependent on them; blacks to date, do not have an economical base. Slavery began in 1619 and was legalized in 1641. We were called black gold because we were a free labor force.

Blacks have been bred as individualist. It's not because we don't have the money, but we've been indoctrinated to distrust, making it extremely difficult to work together. We leave our communities to buy what we need, but there was a time when we had stores within our own communities: laundry mats, furniture stores, cab companies, restaurants, food stores, and even our own bus stations. When I was in the pastorate everybody wanted to preach. They would get mad when you refused to let them preach. They would come in and tell you how the church should operate. Then, I would see some of those same ones join the white church, sit down and do whatever the white pastor told them to do. The slave mentality remains in effect.

They would sit for years and not say a word. They won't even tell the Pastor they're called to preach, but as soon as they join the black church they quickly say, "I've received the call." I know pastors who have lost their church and are now sitting under other pastors. They are doing nothing, and don't see wrong in their choice. But, if God called you, why aren't you doing what he's called you to? This is not a racist message, but it is an observation of things I have experienced.

Society has not helped. We must help ourselves. Civil rights? We can ride the bus, but we are not given equal and equitable opportunity to own it. We can shop stores, but we are not qualified to own one. Other ethnic groups come into our communities, place bars around their stores, and profit on us spending our money, purchasing black products from their stores. And they do not support black owned businesses in these same communities. How do other ethnic groups come into our communities and we support them, but we are reluctant and even opposed to supporting our own? There is a strong spirit of division sown within the black community, and the Willie Lynch letter and method holds true today.

The black man was stripped of his identity, and along with his lost identity, he has also lost his power. The black man needs to find himself. Not only has predicament impacted our community but it has also affected the way we operate in God's church. I've never witnessed so many women pastors, bishops, and apostles. And despite all, there's no scripture to support this. We are disconnected from God and don't know it. The Bible tells the woman, the Holy women of God, that you have the authority to help get that man where he needs to be. Now he needs a help mate. He needs someone to help him. Peter says, *Likewise, ye wives, be in subjections to their own husbands; that, if any obey not the word, they also may without the word be won by the conversation of the wives; I Peter 3:1* Women you have great influence when you're led by the Word of God. You don't have to continue to be affected by a letter or things that were meant to keep us down as a race. Help your man, your husband, find his identity by being the woman of God described in *Titus 2:3-5*.

ROLE REVERSAL - THE MAN AND WOMAN

Galatians 3:1 *O foolish Galatians, who hath bewitched you, that ye should not obey the truth, before whose eyes Jesus Christ hath been evidently set forth, crucified among you?*

I'd like to say to the church of believers, many of which have been turned away, who bewitched you to turn away from the Lord? During the period of Barak Obama's presidency of the United States, he misled America by professing to be a Christian. He came into office claiming he did not believe in same sex marriage, but because he listened to his wife, children, friends, and other officials, he changed his belief. He went against the Word of God and sanctioned same sex marriage. This act was an abomination against God. He became the first president to back marriages publicly for gays, lesbians, and transgender. President Obama opened a serious door of immorality and choices that were blasphemous!

This is the same thing Adam did in the Garden of Eden. God did not directly reprimand Adam about eating the fruit before he addressed his hearkening to the voice of his wife. Genesis 3:17 This is what many preachers do today: Listen to man rather than to God. When people start talking to you listen carefully and you will hear, "Well, I feel, I think, or I believe." If we are Christians, we should always say what the scriptures says. Because Adam hearkened to the voice of his wife and ate of the tree which God commanded him not to eat, the ground was cursed. And the same happens to us when we listen to people more than we listen to God.

Many preachers have the Bruce Jenner anointing where they turn themselves into something different than who they were created. Bruce Jenner changed his name to Caitlyn Jenner, but he was born Bruce Jenner on October 28, 1949. He was a well-known track and field athlete and Reality TV Star. He was a gold medalist winner, setting a world record in the decathlon at the 1976 Summer Olympics. He played football in college but had an injury that forced him to leave the sport and pursue track and field. But in 2015, Bruce announced to the world that he was a transgender. He identified himself as a woman and would no longer be living as Bruce Jenner. Bruce received hormone treatments along with many anatomical surgical changes to present himself as Caitlyn Jenner. But when Bruce stands before God, even though he had some body changes, which he made not God, God will say, "Bruce, I know that's you."

Like Bruce, many preachers today are trying to make themselves something God didn't. Believers! Body of Christ! Who has bewitched you to believe a lie? We are disconnected and don't even know it. Many may be thinking that I have something against people who have chosen to live gay, lesbian, transgender, or bi-sexual lifestyles. You would be wrong. During my pastorate there were those who chose these same lifestyles and attended my church. I preached the word to them like I did everyone else. We are commanded to love people as Christ did. They have rights just like everyone else. If they desire a career, they should be able to work and fulfill their careers like everyone else. They should have equal opportunities and not be discriminated against. According to the scriptures however, I don't agree with their lifestyle. They have a right to believe what they believe, as I have the same rights to do and believe what the scriptures teach.

I don't believe in prostitution. I don't agree with polygamy. I don't agree with pedophilia or anything vulgar. I don't believe people should engage intimately with animals either. God gives us the commandment in His Word to love one another as He loves us. I don't agree with the lifestyle or sinful behavior, but I have been called to love the person; not the sin. If you are summoned to court, tried, and found guilty or innocent, the outcome is determined by the preponderance of evidence presented. My evidence regarding these lifestyle choices are found in *Genesis 19* and *Leviticus 18*. Read about Sodom and Gomorrah. I didn't make this stuff up, it's in the Bible. It doesn't matter if our laws change. And it doesn't matter what people say or think. God does not change. He is the same today, yesterday and forever more. *Hebrews 13:8* Case Closed!

Scripture References: *Romans 1:26-28, Jude 1:7-8, 1Timothy 8-10, Mark 10:6-9, I Corinthians 7:2, I Corinthians 6:9-11, Leviticus 18:22, I Corinthians 6:17-20 Leviticus 20:13, and Matthew 19:4-6*

I didn't say these things; they are published in God's

Word! *We are Disconnected and Don't Know It*! Again, our former President Barak Obama said these things were okay and placed them into law, but this does not make it okay according to the Scriptures. God said I am the Lord thou God and I change not. When Obama made this a law it was an abomination. The order of God was and remains male and female. I haven't seen where He made anything else.

Pastors, evangelist, bishops, preachers, deacons, and even doctors of the Gospel must be very careful how we are promoted by people around us. Unfortunately, people see more of us than they see of Jesus, and this is dangerous. I've heard many pastors say they are the pastor and founder of a church. Well, these are the words of Christ according to *Matthew 16:18*: *And I say also unto thee, That thou art Peter, and upon this rock I will build my church; and the gates of hell shall not prevail against it.* The Lord Himself said upon this rock I build my church. We work for Jesus. But out of the Pastors own mouths they say they are the pastor and founders of their church. When this is said, it is an outright lie. You may be the pastor, but you are not the founder.

The Church originated in Acts on the day of Pentecost. *Acts 2* and *John 20:21-22* The writer John pens these words, *Believest thou not that I am in the Father, and the Father in me? The words that I speak unto you I speak not of myself: but the Father that dwelleth in me, He doeth the works. Believe me that I am in the Father, and the Father in me: or else believe me for the very works' sake.* John

14:10-11 I repeat, if the Bible doesn't say it, we can't say it. We should say what the Bible says. If Jesus said he built his church, how can we say we are the founders? Anyone who says they are the founders of the church is making an incorrect statement. Let me tell the truth: They are wrong. (Well let me just tell the butt naked truth: they're lying according to the Word of God.)

Deuteronomy 4:2 says, *Ye shall not add unto the word which I command you, neither shall ye diminish ought from it, that ye may keep the commandments of the Lord your God which I command you.* In Acts 3, there was a man who was lame from his mother's womb and he was laid daily at the temple's gate asking alms from the people who entered. When he saw Peter and John approaching the temple, he asked them for alms. (Alms is money or food given to poor people. We see a lot of this today when we see people begging on the street.) Wouldn't it be a powerful display of Gods' love if we operated the way they did during Biblical times? Peter and John told the lame, "Silver and gold have I none; but such as I have given I thee: In the name of Jesus Christ of Nazareth rise up and walk." Immediately that man leaped up and began walking.

The Bible says he was walking, leaping and praising God. They moved in the name of Jesus Christ, but the people wanted to look at Peter and John as though they had done a mighty work. In verse 12 Peter saw their response and asked them about their surprise? Or, why are you looking at us as though we did this by our own power or holiness? They told them, *The God of Abraham,*

Isaac, and of Jacob, the God of our fathers, hath glorified His Son Jesus; whom ye delivered up, and denied him in the presence of Pilate, when he was determined to let him go. Acts 3:13 They took no glory to themselves but gave glory to God with conviction and purity. There was no mess in their hearts. We have subtle ways to take God's glory by saying, "Look what I have done." But we must be careful how we allow people to view us; calling us in manners that God does not call us.

We want to be important knowing the things that exists within us, but this takes the attention away from God. Then, we begin taking the credit for ourselves; that's a dangerous thing. Whenever God gives us an assignment, he does not give us roles and feats we can do alone. If you work for a company, you cannot make changes to the rules established by the organization. My friend Anna is the owner of her company; Shelia works for her. The organization has a dress code, specific work hours, and an established wage for each employee. Anna went on a three-month vacation and while away, Shelia changed the dress code, work schedule and pay grade for every employee without proper authorization. She is no longer following Anna's example, so what do you suppose the owner's response will be once she has returned? I asked Anna what she would do to Shelia and her response was, "She got to go!"

Much like Anna and Shelia, Christ left us in charge, so the same should occur. *And he said unto them, Go ye into all the world, and preach the gospel to every creature.*

Mark 16:15 And in *Matthew 28:19* he said, *Go ye therefore, and teach all nations, baptizing them in the name of the Father, and of the Son, and of the Holy Ghost.* These are the instructions Christ gave us. We do not have the right to change things. Just as Paul charged Timothy, *I charge thee therefore before God, and the Lord Jesus Christ, who shall judge the quick and the dead at his appearing and his kingdom; Preach the word; be instant in season, out of season; reprove, rebuke, exhort with all longsuffering and doctrine. For the time will come when they will not endure sound doctrine; but after their own lusts shall they heap to themselves teachers, having itching ears:* II Timothy 4:1-3

Just because you call yourself an apostle, minister, pastor, preacher, bishop, deacon or deaconess, reverend, doctor, first lady, or any other title you've self-made or given, you do not have the authority to change God's word or plan. So many want a title. Take the garbage man. We all know he's a garbage man because of what he does, but we don't go around calling him "Garbage Man." You may say, "Hey, Mr. Garbage Man, but that's his title, not his name. He may tell you his name is not garbage man and then tell you his name. Although he may respond to you, he knows his name. You may be successful in a particular area or skill but it doesn't mean you have been called by God to do it. When we stand before God, he will reveal everything about us. Despite how we used his name, he knows what we've been charged to do – authorized and unauthorized. Just like Shelia that worked for Anna. She did not have the authority or permission to change the plans or mode of operation at Anna's company. She messed up Anna's company. You can be successful doing the wrong thing!

MEN ARE OUT OF PLACE

Earlier, I spoke about the way a serpent works. Before a prey is digested the serpent coils itself around the victim, beginning at the head, and squeezes until life has expired. God called man the leader and the head of the house. The strategy has been to remove man from his position; I submit that men are out of place, which has affected our families, communities, churches, and the black men in particular. We must understand the strategy that was intended to move men out of place. Willie Lynch was a tool in the hand of Satan to strategically remove man from the home, their children and households. During slavery, black men were used primarily for breeding. Slave owners wanted black men to make as many babies as possible without any responsibility of caring for them.

Today, many men are making babies, I'm included, without being responsible and taking care of them. I have a relationship with mine today because you can't preach God's Word and deny your children. You are a representative of God. Some men refuse to take care of their babies because they still have that slave mentality. They are not bothered by not being connected with them. It's displayed on TV: children who don't know their father. I tell you, the alleged letters written by Willie Lynch are still at work today. To understand the system implemented by Willie Lynch you must read the letters. The strategy implemented and its affect continues to impact us as men today. The same system is working in the church.

Women have a thing of suspension about "them brothers;" if he doesn't step up, women will say, "I'm married to him but he's not much." Women are placed in situations where they have to do things that they shouldn't. This is because men refuse to stand up and be who they were created to be. Man, you are wrong, and you are out of order. As you read the Willie Lynch letters and understand his strategy, take a good look at the church and our communities. I know women outnumber men, but there is a strong female influence in today's church. There's nothing wrong with women being in the church, but I strongly believe that if a mother has a son and sees another woman dominating her son, that mother would get upset enough to tell her son to stand up and be a man!

This would be the same response of a woman if she witnesses the same being told to her husband. If he is the Pastor of a church but he's not standing up, he would be told, "If God called you to be a Pastor then you need to be a Pastor. Stand up and be a leader. I'm following you and you can't have me doing things that you're supposed to do. That's your job. You're the leader." This is what a woman of God will do. And a man of God will get in his place. Women should be encouraging. She's the helpmate. "Baby this is your job, this is not my job."

A wife should never have to ask her husband to do things like washing the car, cutting grass or painting a room, unless she chooses to do it. And even then, he should help her because that is the order of God and he's leading by example. I believe a woman loves chivalry, and chivalry is not dead! Here you are working, bringing all the money in the house, and he has a piece of a job. If he has one job making a couple hundred dollars then he needs to get another job and do whatever it takes to sustain his family. I would choose to get three jobs before watching my wife work herself ragged and being tired all the time. I'm going to do things to help my wife because I'm a man. Women please hear me and hear me very carefully, if you have a man and you have to tell him to be a man, please understand you do not have a man, you have a boy – he is a child. A man will stand up and be a man!

A godly man will not sit under a woman pastor. He won't do it! This kind of man will discover it's impossible to not be the man. This is what's wrong today: men are out of place and are disconnected from God without knowing it. Men need to stand up and be men in the church. It's easy for people to follow a pastor in a church when he is being led by the Lord. But if you go to a church where the pastor's wife has more influence over him than God has, things will be difficult. I've been in the churches where I've observed the man preaching, while the wife looks at him like we're supposed to be somewhere else, like K&W, in about another thirty minutes. Her look could be understood as, "You better bring your message to a close." She has the K & W look, and the next thing you hear him say is, "May the Lord watch between me and thee while we're absent one from another, Amen." And with that, he quickly dismisses church.

Men need to get in order because there are too many mothers, grandmothers, and aunties that are stunting the growth of our young men and preventing their development. Young men are looking for mommas; someone to cook and clean for them, buy their clothes and clothe them, and this prevents their evolution into real men. They have the audacity to say they're looking for relationship without understanding fully how to be men. Men are needed to teach their sons and daughters. And much like eagles, men need to experience discomfort. First, the male and female eagles build a nest for their eaglets together (Husband and wife do similar as they train up their children in the way they should go.) The male eagle hunts and provides food for the female and eaglets. Initially, the nest is comfortable, but as the eaglets grow, the parents make the nest less comfortable, removing moss and grass, in order to prepare the eaglets to learn how to fly.

I believe we need to teach our young men how to be providers and protectors, because one day they will be fathers and they can't teach what has not been taught. We, like the eagles, should utilize discomforts to teach our sons how to live, leave, and lead, and not become dependent on the comforts of home. Teach them how to clean, cook, care for the lawns and much more so they can be successful in transitioning into adulthood. Jesus did the same with the disciples. He taught them that life would become uncomfortable one day (Let not your heart be troubled...) He continued to tell them he was going away but would not leave them comfortless. He sent the comforter, the Holy Ghost, to be with them after his departure. The Bible teaches that God watches over His Word. He watches everything we do. Slavery was and is horrendous. It messed us up, the victims up, and has corrupted our society.

God has given man the authority to walk in Jesus' name. Therefore, when God directs us to speak or act on his behalf, we should tell the people we're doing it for him. I have never asked the church how to be a pastor or how I should serve the church. I've always worked with the vision and assignment of God. Much like God gave Moses a vision for Israel, the vision remained the same after Moses' death. It did not change because Joshua was his successor. Before his death, Moses told the spies to scout out the land of Canaan. They returned talking about giants and gave an evil report. They changed the vision of Canaan, not God. God's words are constant: They never change. So, respect and honor your wife, but do not change what God says for her or anyone else.

I've heard women say, "I'm just as much a man as he is." What she is doing is taking his manhood and putting it into her jewelry box. You may ask your pastor if he's alright, but in instances like this, the wife has taken away his manhood. He has relinquished his power similar to Adam in the Garden of Eden. God punished the serpent and Eve, but when He punished Adam He said the following: *And unto Adam he said, Because thou hast hearkened unto the voice of thy wife, and hast eaten of the tree, of which I commanded thee, saying, Thou shalt not eat of it: cursed is the ground for thy sake; in sorrow shalt thou eat of it all the days of thy life. Genesis 3:17* The reason for God's response was because Adam was the one in charge, not Eve. If she had the same assignment God would have said the same to both Adam and Eve.

Listen and receive from your wife if she is compliant with God's Word. If she is not, it is a dangerous thing for your spiritual growth. The Bible states, *(For if a man know not how to rule his own house, how shall he take care of the church of God?) I Timothy 3:5* You are the head of the house. And the scripture says the same for Bishops and Deacons. It also says your children should be in subjection to the word. If you are the pastor of a church and your children are out of order – they are all over the church causing disruption; disrespectful, and you're talking about you are a preacher? Oh, no. This is a sign you have come up with that Bruce Jenner spirit: Turning yourself into something God did not call. Bruce said he did it; he said he was very unhappy with his life. God's man is going to stand up and also tell others how to stand. *Ephesians 6*

God calls men as leaders, as he placed them as leaders of their own house. Men do not wait until they are married before becoming the head, they began this role as a child and develop into young adulthood. They are trained to lead before they reach adult age. Women alike, do not wait until they are married before becoming a wife. Look at what the scripture says, *Whoso findeth a wife findeth a good thing and obtained favor of the Lord. Proverbs 18:22* Sisters possess the characteristics of a wife before she meets you.

Don't be like me. Stevie Wonder could sing but he couldn't see a lick. I'm saying there was a time that I was like Stevie Wonder. I could sing fairly well, but I had problems seeing. I said, "Lord, restore my sight." I was like Blind Bartimus. The Lord asked, "What do you want, Gwat?" I said, "That I may receive my sight." My sight has messed me up, Lord! I was attracted to physical appearances, and I was drawn away of my own lust and enticed. And I behaved like the old gospel song whenever I saw a certain physical type: "That's good enough for me."

POWER, MONEY, AND LOVE

I Timothy 6:10 *For the love of money is the root of all evil: which while some coveted after, they have erred from the faith, and pierced themselves through with many sorrow.*

Mark 8:36-37 *For what shall it profit a man, if he shall gain the whole world, and lose his soul? Or what shall a man give in exchange for his soul?*

On TV, evangelists are saying all kinds of things. In times past, preachers spoke the Word of God, but now many are merely motivational speakers. The first time I preached was in a storefront church and they gave me a dollar for my services, and I was so excited. The next church where I preached, I gave that same dollar in the offering. It was not about the money; I was so excited to tell people about Jesus. I recall, the first church of my pastorate, a lady who gave me a check for $10,000.00 and told me to use it any way I wanted. I could have kept all or part of the money, but instead I gave it all to the church. There was a church that asked me to preach a revival for them, and it was three hours away, one-way. As I stated earlier, I have never charged to preach anywhere because I worked outside of the church. At the end of the week-long revival, the pastor gave me $125.00. This did not cover the cost of gas or cleaners spent for the week. The host pastor asked me to come again and I told him I would, because it wasn't about the money.

During my pastorate another church presented me with a fifth Sunday offering and I turned it down. (You will not find many preachers who will do this.) The fifth Sunday offering was fairly substantial, but again God didn't call me to preach for the money. I asked for the allegiance of the people to do what God called me to do – win souls; work for the kingdom. I was not for sale. When money is your motivation, it's a dangerous thing. When you do not accept speaking engagements without knowing the amount you will be paid, you are seriously in trouble. I have known many preachers that are motivated by money. They will not preach at your church unless you provide hotel accommodation, plane tickets, and meals for them and their entourage. It's a dangerous thing when money is more important than winning souls. For many preachers, money motivates everything they do.

There was a king in the Old Testament named Ahab, and he was one of the worse kings to live because of his wicked wife Jezebel. *I King 21:1-16* Ahab listened to the voice of his wife, which resulted in him worshipping the idol god, Ba'al. Jezebel was known for killing in order to get what she wanted. One day, her husband, King Ahab was stricken with sadness and refused to eat. Jezebel did not understand why his spirit was so sad. Ahab told her it was because he'd spoken to Naboth, the Jezreelite, requesting to purchase his vineyard or exchange it for another, but he refused. Jezebel reminded Ahab that he governed the kingdom of Israel and told him to eat and be merry.

Additionally, she said she would get Naboth's vineyard. So, she wrote letters in Ahab's name, sealed them with his seal, and sent them to the chief men of the city where Naboth lived to have him stoned. After his death, she told Ahab to go and take the vineyard; this is why I say when money or power controls you it's a dangerous thing.

I've rebuked my wife in front of preachers while in my church office. As I remember, she walked in my office to rebuke me for bringing the homeless to church. As the pastor, I immediately corrected her openly. A wife should be a blessing to you, as mentioned in Proverbs 31. On the other hand, she can be like Jezebel, or like Rebekah, Isaac's wife who overheard him talking to their eldest son Esau. When Isaac was in old age and his eyes dim, his wife manipulated and conspired against his plans. It's a dangerous thing when you have a woman who knows how to make good stew. It can mess a man up. Rebekah plotted by cooking a stew on behalf of her favorite son, Jacob. She showed Jacob how to get his brothers birthright and "first born" blessing which belonged to Esau. Watch out for the stew!

In the Garden of Eden, Adam was living in utopia; everything was perfect. He had a health plan, he was going to live forever, and everything he needed was at his fingertip. Then, he listened to the woman instead of God. And in an instance, he and his wife were living in a homeless shelter. A woman can be a blessing or a very dangerous thing, especially when she can cook and make a good pot of stew. A relationship with the wrong man or woman can and has caused chaos and destruction in the church. (I'll say a strong "AMEN" to that!)

Where are the Jeremiahs of today? People say they are apostles, but where are those who warn the people? *Malachi 2:1-9* I am not charging every preacher, because there are preachers who are feeding the sheep and not fleecing them. These are a light in the world; like a city set on a hill. My doctor told me that I need to leave salt alone because salt is not good for you, but I said, "I read the Bible and God said salt is good for me. God said I was the salt of the earth. I understand what the doctor meant, but God looks at salt differently. The Word teaches us that we are the salt of the earth, and the problem with many is the salt has lost its savor. There is no seasoning in the earth, and the unfortunate commentary is we as Christians, like a saltshaker, are not shaking salt for the world.

We are the seasoning of the earth. Jesus said, we are the light of the world. These are the two special things God told us to be: salt and light. Sometimes people say it's dark out here (in this world.) Why does it feel this way? What's wrong with this here? People ask, "What's wrong with the world today?" What are they actually asking? Are they asking where is the salt? What's wrong with people; why is the church in such condition? They're saying, there's no salt! Or, dawg, the preacher didn't preach anything today. What's being said is he does not have any salt in him - there's no salt and no light. In essence, *We are Disconnected and Don't Know It!!*

Churches are inhaling but they are not exhaling.

People are going to church seeking answers and are being comforted in their sins. Church leaders are more concerned about the traditions of men rather than spiritual truth; promoting Santa Claus and Christmas trees, the Easter Bunny and dyed eggs, and so forth. Everybody knows that rabbits don't lay eggs, but they will give you the eggs to hide for the children to find. When King Agrippa asked the people who they wanted to be freed, Barabbas or Jesus, the chief priests and elders persuaded the crowd to ask for Barabbas and destroy Jesus. They wanted Barabbas, the criminal, to be set free. They could have asked for Jesus, but they asked for Barabbas instead. *Matthew 27: 17-26*

The main objective should be to prepare people for the coming of the Lord Jesus Christ. The Bible says, *And, behold, I come quickly; and my reward is with me, to give every man according as his work shall be. Revelation 22:12* It also states, *He that is unjust, let him be unjust still: and he which is filthy, let him be filthy still: and he that is righteous, let him be righteous still: and he that is holy, let him be holy still. Revelation 22:11* In other words, there will be a time when it's too late for change to occur. So, with love I would say, Repent and be baptized in the name of Jesus Christ for the remission of sins, and ye shall receive the gift of the Holy Spirit. Please understand these are not my words but the words of Apostle Peter to the church. (Acts 2:38) I encourage you to read the first and second chapters of Acts.

Instead of having Missionary Day, Pastoral or Church Anniversaries, and Founder's Day events, churches should focus on their mission. We create this stuff and choose programs instead of preaching Jesus. We've brought the world into the church, hosting a missionary day without having a mission? Is it just to come together and wear white dresses and fancy shoes? What is the mission? There are churches in Winston Salem that go to the homeless shelter and donate food but will not invite these people to church. They will tell them, "If you want to come to church give us a call;" knowing they are not going to call.

When our church served at the shelter, we didn't tell them to call us if they wanted to visit. We took our vans to the same shelter and picked them up and fed them a hot meal every Sunday following service before returning them. Our people were instructed to love them like we love our own families. That's what they were to us. Family. Love is an action word, so we demonstrated our love. Zacchaeus, the rich tax collector, sought to see Jesus, because of his short statue he was unable to view him through the crowd. Undeterred, he ran and climbed the sycamore tree to view Jesus, and when Jesus saw him, he said, *Zacchaeus, make haste, and come down; for today I must abide at thy house. Luke 19:7b* Jesus mingled with the people; Jesus smelled like the sheep. He cared about the sheep, spent time with them, and they wanted to be around him. When any pastor tells you that he does not care about things that concerns you, he is not acting in accordance with the Word. In Matthew 14, Jesus continued to go forth after hearing of John the Baptist's beheading. The disciples buried his body and traveled by ship to a desert place, while Jesus wanted to be alone. But the people heard he was on the ship and followed him by foot out of the cities.

Jesus never asks anything of us that we are incapable of, nor tell you to do something you can't. If he did, it would mean he's unjust. So, Jesus went forth and ministered to the great multitude. He was moved with compassion toward all and healed the sick. His disciples wanted him to send the people away so they could go into the villages to buy food, but Jesus smelling like his sheep said they need not depart. He told them to feed the people. They responded saying, *We have here but five loaves, and two fishes. Matthew 14:17b* He told the disciples bring them, and he commanded the people to sit down on the grass. He took the five loaves and two fishes, looked up to heaven and blessed them; then he broke each and gave them to his disciples to distribute to the multitude.

Everyone ate until full and had leftovers to remain. This is what a shepherd does: He comes with a solution because he has direct contact with the Father. His job is to take care of the sheep. The scripture says, *Take heed that ye despise not one of these little ones; for I say unto you, That in heaven their angels do always behold the face of my Father which is in heaven. For the Son of man is come to save that which was lost. How think ye? If a man have a hundred sheep, and one of them be gone astray, doth he not leave the ninety and nine, and goeth into the mountains, and seeketh that which is gone astray? And if so be that he find it, verily I say unto you, he rejoiceth more of that sheep, than of the ninety and nine which went not astray. Even so it is not the will of your Father which is in heaven, that one of these little ones should perish. Matthew 18:10-14*

You are not a true pastor if you are not caring for the sheep. Sheep need a shepherd. When the shepherd is too busy to care and meet the sheep where they are because of a degree, becoming a reverend, doctor, bishop, apostle or evangelist, then your calling has erred. If you are too busy when a church can't afford you (because you come with a price,) you have not been called by God to lead his sheep. You will answer to God and *You are Disconnected and Don't Even Know It!*

MODERN DAY CHURCH

Growing up, when my momma would by my church clothes, she would say, "These are your church clothes," and I understood they were not to be worn for anything else. We had church clothes and play clothes, but you never mixed the two. If there was a storm, thundering and lightening, momma would tell everybody in the house to sit down, be quiet, and turn off the lights. The Lord was working, and we had to be still. She taught us things I didn't understand until I got saved. The Bible says, *The fear of the Lord is the beginning of wisdom: a good understanding have all they that do his commandments: his praise endureth forever. Psalm 111:10* Failure to fear the Lord would mean the death of me. It was a respect and reverence for God that my momma taught me.

She taught us to reverence and fear God's house; you did not go to God's house acting any kind of way. My mom would be singing in the choir and lock eyes with me and I knew not to move. We did not run in church, we used the restroom before church started, and if any other need arose, I knew to hold it until service had ended. There was no getting up and moving around during church: We did not do that. And if you act up in church, you were taken outside, whipped, and brought back inside. You would be sniffling and making all kind of noise. This was a Baptist church, but you would probably be speaking in tongues if it was a Holiness church. My momma would tell me to stop sniffling and making a bunch of noise after she whipped you half to death. I would sit down and say nothing.

Kids today are much different. I have seen pastors whose children were disruptive and running around in the church, while he and his wife sat without saying anything. There used to be a respect for God's house, but today we are *Disconnected and Don't Know It!* Where is the reverence for God today? Women wore hats to church and kept their heads covered. Women never wore pants; they didn't come with their breast out. And if a woman was out of order, the Mothers of the Church quickly corrected them. Now, women come to church dressing sensual, with the purpose of looking sexy, looking for a man. Where are the Church Mothers? If your dress was too short or you showed too much cleavage, the Mothers would give you a scarf or something and tell you to cover up. These are things I witnessed as a kid, but this new generation of preachers have created their own doctrine – calling bad good, and good evil.

A large congregation does not mean you're walking with God. Christ warns us, *Enter ye in at the strait gate: for wide is the gate, and broad is the way, that leadeth to destruction, and many there be which go in there at: Because strait is the gate, and narrow is the way, which leadeth unto life, and few there be that find it. Matthew 7:13-14* You can be a believer and not be saved. I love to read from the King James Version, but I encourage you to read II Corinthians 4. It tells us how we should handle ourselves, and that none of us preach ourselves or for ourselves. We preach Christ Jesus. I acknowledge that we live in a new day and things have changed, but the Bible says, *Jesus Christ the same yesterday, and today, and forever. Hebrews 13:8* God doesn't change.

Churches are organized where pastors go to conference and pay for a message from God. Then, the pastors give you your message, but you have to pay for it. You have to pay $995.00 for something that is free. I have gone to these types of conferences, and the more money you give or pay determines where you sit at the head table. If you give enough in donations or fees, they will give back to you because they want to keep the money coming. Greed is a hell of a thing. We attend these conferences and return to our churches with nothing for the people. Pastors glean from other pastors who know nothing about your sheep instead of going to the Master Shepherd. We seek and run after what Christ offers us freely. He promised the Holy Spirit would lead and direct us into all truth. *John 14:11-21* Christ speaks in these verses of His presence in our lives. Preachers are seeking from one another what they should seek from God.

During my younger years I worked for R. J. Reynolds Tobacco Company. They trained me to do various jobs. Most companies, after they hire you, will provide on the job training. God does the same. When he calls you, he trains or prepares you for the job. Paul was schooled by the Holy Ghost. God taught him. He is quoted saying, *For I neither received it of man, neither was I taught it, but by the revelation of Jesus Christ. Galatians 1:12* Paul goes further to say, *Neither went I up to Jerusalem to them which were apostles before me; but I went into Arabia, and returned again unto Damascus. Galatians 1:17* When God calls, he also prepares you. Man can teach you philosophy and theology, but it takes God to anoint you to teach and preach, as one who has the authority of God.

Pastors pay other pastors to teach them about their sheep, while they take their money and buy themselves bigger jets, houses and cars. Look at your sheep? How have they benefited from these conferences? How many additional souls have been saved since you've received their knowledge from the round table? Most did not even get their money's worth. Every conference I attended, I never went for the preacher to tell me about my church because God had already given me the vision for the people assigned to me. Some pastors will fleece their sheep in order to get to a conference, only to return empty handed. All you did was take a vacation.

Preachers preach as though money and prosperity validates their walk with Christ. Nowhere in the Bible do you find where Jesus preached a message of prosperity. He preached about the lost; I can show you that. He preached about love; I can show you that. He preached about forgiveness; I can show you that. He preached about holy living; I can show you that. He preached about prayer; I can show you that too. *Matthew 21:12-14; Mark 11:15-18; John 2:14-16; Matthew 12.* Jesus went into the temple of God and cast out those that bought and sold there. Jesus turned over the tables of the money changers and the seats of those who sold doves. Jesus declared, *And said unto them, It is written, My house shall be called the house of prayer; but ye have made it a den of thieves.* Matthew 21:13 What have we allowed in the Lord's church? Consider what he would come through and clean from his house today? Once Jesus drove out the money changers and sellers, the temple was returned to a place of worship.

If you are one of those preachers who lead a family church, or you get upset when tithers asked about the finances of the church, then you already know the church is yours and not God. God has nothing to do with the church you created. Jesus allowed the lame and the blind to come and he healed them. The temple was a place to come and receive healing from God. It was a place of refuge, prayer, and praise and worship. Make sure you are not one of the many. If you are an apostle, what is the message you are delivering to keep the church in order? Modern day apostles would have asked, "Who said anything about prosperity? This is not in the Bible." O, Modern Church, who has bewitched you?

The church has gotten caught up in denominationalism, and this is another means of separating the Body of Christ. We have too much segregation in our churches. We can't come together as a body because everyone wants to be chief. This is also why we have churches on every street corner. The church has become a family business. We put our family members in positions that God has not called, and leaders call them because they can keep it all in the family. You know you are in trouble when the pastor and his family controls most or all aspects of the church. The Holy Spirit takes a back seat. We need to understand that as God adds qualified people to the body, they should be in place to lead as well.

During biblical times, the apostles preach the same message. They didn't set up denominations: Baptist, Methodist, Catholics, Mormons, Apostolic, Church of God in Christ, Jehovah's Witnesses, Primitive Baptist, Pentecostals, etc. This was the start of the church disconnectedness. In Acts 2, we read about the fellowship of the believers. Paul said they continued steadfastly in the apostles' doctrines and fellowship and in breaking of bread and in prayers; saints had all things in common. In my reading of the scriptures they went from city to city and they preached the same message. Today, we have some baptizing new believers in the name of the Father, Son, and Holy Ghost, others in the name of Jesus, more in the name of Jesus Christ, while others sprinkle. But I submit unto you again, they were steadfast in the Apostle's doctrine – this was the teaching of Jesus Christ. They preached the same message and walked in the name of Jesus.

Their battle cry was "Repent every one of you and be baptized in the name of Jesus Christ and ye shall receive the gift of the Holy Ghost." So, when people say in the name of the Father, the Son, and the Holy Ghost, I'm reminded, his name is not Father; and it is not Son. Jesus was the Father in the flesh. Jesus said, *Believest thou not that I am in the Father, and the Father in Me? The words that I speak unto you I speak not of myself: but the Father that dwelleth in me, he doeth the works.* John 14:10 The Holy Spirit works the same in believers today by leading us in the things of God.

Jesus further states, *And I will pray the Father, and he shall give you another Comforter, that he may abide with you forever. Even the Spirit of truth; whom the world cannot receive, because it seeth him not, neither knoweth him: but ye know him; for he dwelleth with you and shall be in you. I will not leave you comfortless: I will come to you. Yet a little while, and the world seeth me no more; but ye see me: because I live, ye shall live also. At that day ye shall know that I am in my Father, and ye in me, and I in you. He that hath my commandments, and keepeth them, he it is that loveth me: and he that loveth me shall be loved of my Father, and I will love him, and will manifest myself to him.* John 14:16-21 Believers we need to be obedient to God's Word and stay connected.

MARRIAGE

I have made a lot of mistakes and learned from my wrongs. Married twice: I sincerely wanted my first marriage to work, but after it ended, I never wanted to marry again. We were married for many years, and like most, I wanted it to last forever. I knew God hated divorce. So, if you cannot live with your spouse, then you should remain single. *Malachi 2:15-16* God watched how I treated his daughter. I realize my first marriage did not work because I didn't want it to, but because I, like the people of God, perished for the lack of knowledge. *Hosea 4:6* I did not have the knowledge needed to sustain a good marriage. I knew how to tie my shoes, dress myself, and feed myself, but there were spiritual things concerning my life, family, and other situations that I did not. I was still learning about God and those things relating to spiritual development and relationships.

I did not know how to deal well, lacking this information, because many times my flesh got in the way of God. I had not learned knowledge about how to make my marriage work, but once I learned, I returned to her and asked if we could try again. I sought God for understanding and he taught me how to be a better husband, but she was still in the same place. And because of this, we were unable to walk together as the Bible declares. *Can two walk together, except they agreed? Amos 3:3* I had agreed to God's Word, but she had to agree as well in order for us to make it as a couple. My marriage dissolved; my children were impacted. I am still influenced by the affects today.

I loved the women I was married to, but to this day, I do not agree with the way they functioned. I have a problem when spouses don't exhibit conduct after the Word of God. God's Word is our navigational system and it teaches us how we are to behave and nurture marital relationships. When we refuse to listen to God, we set ourselves up for defeat. That's why the scripture says, *My people are destroyed for lack of knowledge: because thou has rejected knowledge, I will also reject thee. Hosea 4:6a* We cannot put off studying. The scriptures also say, *Study to shew thyself approved unto God, a workman that needeth not to be ashamed, rightly dividing the word of truth. II Timothy 2:15* I don't have to be ashamed to answer you because I know how to rightly divide the words of truth. Because I can rightly divide the Word of God, I am able to operate as God directs. I don't know everything about the Bible, but concerning life, I know he empowers me. He never tells me to walk, live, or love a certain way without giving me the ability to succeed.

God is just and fair. He never asks us beyond our means. God showed me how to be a husband; he gave me power to lead as well. According to scriptures, I was told to love my wife, my children, and to be patient with her, as she was the weaker vessel. He showed me things about her, and said I was the head of the house, Christ was head over me, and I was the head over my wife. I was not told to dominate or control my wife, and I could not love him without loving her. I understood if I loved God the right way, I could love my wife the same. I had to make sure I was loving God: representing and respecting him; so, when I went to her, I attempted to tell her what God shared with me from the scriptures. The first thing Jesus taught about love consisted of two commandments: *And thou shalt love the Lord thy God with all thy heart, and with all thy soul, and with all thy mind, and with all thy strength: this is the first commandment. And the second is like, namely this, Thou shalt love thy neighbor as thyself. There is none other commandment greater than these. Matthew 12:30-31*

    Every question can be answered by God's Word. As you walk in God's Word, knowledge is given on how you should love and live with her. If we are not listening to God, it is even more difficult to listen to your spouse. I am very illiterate or unskilled with the use of a computer, but others are more knowledgeable than I. They have a greater knowledge and are capable of teaching me and others, on how to use the computer. Relationships are the same. God is willing to teach us the best knowledge about sustaining great relationships. At some point in my spiritual life I was unable to grow and develop more. He said anything you ask in my name, I will give it to you. John 15:16 This is when I went to my heavenly Father and asked, "Lord, I do not have knowledge in this area. Please show me what I need to do. How do I do this?" God was responsible and obligated to help me get through it, and he showed me how to deal with my first wife.

After our separation, I wanted my marriage restored. I reached out to my wife, I took her to dinner, doctor appointments, bought her medicine, dated her again, and helped her with anything she needed. I never turned my back on her. After all of this, she would not respond to reconciling our marriage. I asked her what I had done so bad that we couldn't get back together again? I told her God showed me what I needed to do to be a better husband. I was now walking in it. But God would not force her to walk into anything she did not want. God doesn't override our will. Even though my heart was right: I was not abusive, and I did not mistreat her, yet she was unwilling. I explained my conduct was a result of influences from ministry. I learned I was under attack due to my witnessing and preaching on the streets. People were talking about me, I was stampeding the gates of hell, and I was a threat to the devil's kingdom. Consequently, Satan was now attacking me, my marriage and family.

I also learned Satan was not attacking people who weren't doing anything. Those sitting on Hallelujah Boulevard were not suffering attack. Although I was out doing witnessing, I always took time to be with my wife. I remember our children tried to encourage her to participate with me, but she wasn't willing. I really believe Satan used her to get to me: To shut me down and discourage me. I was in a place with God where I had not been before. Many times, the enemy came very strategically, using the people closest to me to weaken my spiritual life. He was having a serious effect on my life. Despite my telling her what the Bible says, she did not want to hear it. I loved my wife and wanted my first marriage to work. I did not want a divorce, but my wife had to want it as well. I couldn't fight alone.

I fathered children before I got married, as she was aware, and we shared children together following marriage. I could not get up and preach to others and treat my children like outcasts. I knew I had to treat all of my children fairly, but my greatest problem was I married a woman who wanted me without these children. But they were mine, and they were my responsibility before I met her. After we married, she presented conditions regarding the children. I knew if I wanted God to use me it would be contingent on the way I treat my children, all of them, and my wife. So, I tried to get my wife to understand that we were representing God and not ourselves. God was watching our conduct. The both of us needed ears to hear the Word of God. We had to do right as a couple. Problems occur when the two cannot agree.

God gives us knowledge about life, but it's our choice to accept or reject it. Like the man at the pool of Bethesda, the Lord knew he was in bad shape when Jesus came up to him. Jesus asked if he wanted his help, but the man kept talking about his condition. John 5:1-9 And in my marriage, I asked God to help us get through the problems surrounding my children. My wife kept talking about my children and problems. It was only a problem because of the way she looked at it. When she married me, she married a man that was born in sin and shaped in iniquity, but God saved me. I was now attempting to walk in righteousness with

God. But I married someone who loved God but loved me with limitations. She loved me until it came to my children. My children were a part of me, and they were non-negotiable. We eventually divorced and I lived alone for many years.

Then, I allowed the influence of people to disrupt my life. I was fine as single man, and I learned to trust God. He did not send anyone, and I wasn't looking. It was clear to me if God did not sanction marriage, I did not want it. But there are always people who thought more highly of themselves than they should – I call them Cupids. People started telling me, "Well, you know you are by yourself. And you need someone." I had been divorced for many years. Friends and others started telling me I needed a wife. People told me they had someone they wanted me to meet, and I started listening. Satan always sends us the stuff we like; he knew what I liked. I said earlier I've made some mistakes in my life. My flesh started calling me "Gwat," and I was drawn away of my own lust and enticed.

I knew I was in trouble when my flesh started calling me Gwat! I said, "Look a there, look a there..." It wasn't the Holy Ghost; it was the Lust Ghost. I was drawn away of my own lust. *But every man is tempted, when he is drawn away of his own lust, and enticed. James 1:14* One of Satan's main objectives is to influence the man of God away from their assignment. Satan is a strategist; I knew he was after me. He'd been tracking me for a long time. I listened to people and my flesh, and I can't blame anyone. I was drawn away and tempted. I married again but I was wrong. I have apologized to my second wife. She was a nice person but sometimes you do things without truly being ready. Today, if I could be of help to her, I would, but I wished I had not interrupted her life. I should never have gotten married a second time. I should have remained single and unmarried.

I WANNA BE SOMETHING

There are many people who, like Bruce Jenner, made up their mind that that they are not satisfied being who they are. Despite his Olympic medals, football career, and notoriety for winning the men's decathlon, he was unhappy and wanted to be someone else (other than the person God created.) He decided to be Caitlyn Jenner and identify himself as a woman. Many preachers today wrestle with the same. They try and make themselves to be someone God didn't make. Many people today are not satisfied with how God created them. They go to great lengths to be someone other than themselves. I just wanted to be saved. I did not want to go to hell. I didn't have to be a preacher, deacon, or live with any kind of title. I was happy knowing God had changed my life, and I rejoiced about that. I knew I had really changed.

I did not tell anyone I was a preacher, but I gave my testimony. I was like the woman at the well whom he told to go and tell the people what I did for you. I gave my testimony and told how God changed my life. I didn't seek to be anything more: not a preacher or an evangelist. I didn't care about anything else; I was glad to be saved. My positions and calling were God's doing, but it was not my choice. I was just so happy to be safe in His arms. I was thirty-seven when I accepted my first pastorate. So, for thirteen years, I learned from brothers who were seasoned in the gospel. I spent time with such leaders: Rev. Rice, (Mercy Seat), Pastor Joseph Samuels (St Stephens Baptist Church), Rev. Sallie (Morningside Baptist Church), Rev. Mack (Emmanuel Baptist Church), Pastor Charles Leak (Phillips Chapel), Pastor Noah King (Lula Street COG), and Minister Charlie Clemmons (Street Ministers). These were pastors and ministers of honor, and I learned from them. They gave me godly counsel and I applied their wisdom to my life.

Young pastors today, it's difficult to tell them much. They have a "You can't tell me nothing" anointing. They know everything about everything. They are quick to say, "I got this." I am now seventy- two years of age, and I've learned that God does not give you any assignment to do alone. You will always need someone's help, and if you notice, your blessing is always in someone else's mouth. Now, with love and respect, this is only for those who have an ear to hear. Many young pastors today do not have an ear to hear, they have the "I already know it" anointing. In Matthew 9, Jesus spoke to His disciples and explained, *Then saith he unto his disciples, The harvest truly is plenteous, but the laborers are few; Pray ye therefore the Lord of the harvest, that he will send forth laborers into his harvest. Matthew 9:37-38* There are many brothers and sisters who enjoy the harvest because they understand the mission God gave to the church.

The mission of the church is in *Mark 16:15, And he said unto them, God ye into all the world, and preach the gospel to every creature. He that believeth and is baptized shall be saved; but he that believeth not shall be damned. And these signs shall follow them that believe; In my name shall they cast out devils; they shall speak with new tongues.* As pastors, we are commissioned by God to go into the harvest and labor to win souls for the Kingdom of God. College cannot train you to be a pastor. Some go to school to preach as a career, like many go to school to take up a trade. Some people go to college to become doctors, lawyers, pursue many other career paths.

When God calls you, there is an anointing that is associated with the call and assignment. After some receive titles of pastor, bishop, apostle, doctor, or reverend, they forget where they received it from. Furthermore, they forget about the function of their assignment. They begin thinking of themselves more highly than they ought. *Romans 12:3* Here, we are warned against such thinking. When arrogance is present, and people must go through others to get to you, you are elevating yourself more highly than you ought. And you are of your father, the devil.

When God called Paul as he was nearing his way to Damascus, suddenly a light from heaven shined round about him; he fell to the earth and heard the voice of the Lord calling his name. *Acts 9:3-4* The first thing this did was capture his attention. Paul then had to unlearn everything he thought he knew. (He is an excellent example of how God calls each of us into our assignment.) Then, he had to learn the ways of God: of a pastor, the anointing, responsibility, humility, and servitude. These were some associated responsibilities of his assignment. If God called you to preach, he will also qualify you. He will deprogram and reprogram you to adapt and meet his assignment. He tears down in order to build you up. He takes away the spirit of pride and replaces it with a spirit of humility.

Before entering any branch of the military, you are told they are responsible for your every move: when to get up; when to go to bed. They tell you what to wear and where you can and cannot go. You are their property and you follow their rules and guidelines. Paul experienced the same after his encounter with God. He said, *Though I might also have confidence in the flesh. If any other man thinketh that he hath whereof he might trust in the flesh, I more: Circumcised the eighth day, of the stock of Israel, of the tribe of Benjamin, an Hebrew of the Hebrews; as touching the law, a Pharisee; Concerning zeal, persecuting the church; touching the righteousness which is in the law, blameless, But what things were gain to me, those I counted loss for Christ. Yea doubtless, and I count all things but loss for the excellency of the knowledge of Christ Jesus my Lord: for whom I have suffered the loss of all things, and do count them but dung, that I may win Christ, And be found in him not having mine own righteousness, which is of the law, but that which is through the faith of Christ, the righteousness which is of God by faith. Philippians 3:4-9*

In Galatians 1, Paul certified the brothers that the gospel which was preached to him was not after man. He did not receive it of man, neither was he taught it, but by the revelation of Jesus Christ. *But when it pleased God, who separated me from my mother's womb, and called me by his grace. To reveal his Son in me, that I might preach him among the heathen; immediately I conferred not with flesh and blood: Neither went I up to Jerusalem to them which were apostles before me; but I went into Arabia, and returned again to Damascus. Then after three years I went up to Jerusalem to see Peter, and abode with him fifteen days. Galatians 1:15-18* He did not go to college for another man to teach him. God appointed and anointed him to win souls for the Kingdom.

   I believe many churches today have missed great opportunities in selecting godly leaders, because of the emphasis of educational status instead of the leading of Christ. Jesus said the Spirit of the Lord was upon me. If God calls, he prepares you for your assignment. We have preachers with degrees, using big, eloquent words, but for every big, eloquent word there is the anointing that uses simple words to explain and simplify the message of God in ways a child can understand. Jesus said to feed his sheep; therefore, a pastor's assignment is to make the message of the kingdom understandable to all. To the old and young sheep, a pastor's job is to break down the Word into bit size pieces. It is the pastor's responsibility to make sure all are fed.

   Many things preachers count as gain today, Paul counted them as a loss for Christ. God calls, anoints, and gives each ministry calling their assignment. All belongs to Him, and life is no longer about what we want. Each must do according to *Romans 12: 1-2: I beseech you therefore, brethren, by the mercies of God, that ye present your bodies a living sacrifice, holy, acceptable unto god, which is your reasonable service. And be not conformed to this world: but be ye transformed by the renewing of your mind, that ye may prove what is that good, and acceptable, and perfect, will of God.* Our minds and our hearts are transformed by the Word of God to do his will, and fulfilling his purpose and plan for our lives.

We have not been called to preach prosperity and fame, as the focus must be on the gospel of Christ Jesus. We should not preach for the title, instead we should focus on becoming like Christ, loving people the way he loves us. We are to refrain from anything that draws attention away from God. The ways of the world should be counted as dung, as we strive to operate in the spirit of excellence and knowledge of Jesus Christ, our Lord and Savior. Any desire to be recognized, or an unwillingness to preach without pay, you are a Wannabe. You want to be something; you have become your own God. Novice who think what you do is by your own power, you are thinking more highly of yourself than you should. You need to understand that God never calls anyone to serve alone. Have you called yourself something that God hasn't called you? Are you operating with a spirit of pride? You have not been called to the pastorate and not love the people of God. Pastors take time to know sheep. They spend time together, and sheep learn the voice of the shepherd.

Those called to the pastorate sacrifice and seek lost sheep. If you are too busy to tend the sheep, you are not a pastor. When sheep are sick or hurting, and shepherds neglect tending to the needs of the sheep, you are probably not a pastor. A true pastor serves at all times. Pastors serve all. A true pastor does not serve to receive a paycheck or is not motivated by a salary. Are you in the pastorate for the title? *For we are not as many, which corrupt the word of God: but as of sincerity, but as of God, in the sight of God speak we in Christ. II Corinthians 2:17* Those called by God will, *Cry aloud, spare not, lift thy voice like a trumpet, and shew my people their transgression, and the house of Jacob their sins. Isaiah 58:1*

True pastors do not water down the Word of God or preach feel good messages. They do not allow people to believe going against the Word of God is okay. Again, I have never preached for money. I have never preached as a career. God called me; anointed me to preach the Word – in season and out of season. I pastor everywhere I go and each day of my life. I tell people the truth whether they want it or not. I do not want their blood on my hands, and I want God to trust me. I walk in the authority of Jesus Christ and not in my own. I understand all authority comes from the Father. I have lost many people along the way: people I loved and cared deeply for. I counted the cost and I understood the price as high. I lost everything, and yet I have lost nothing. Above all, I've gained life, strength, and integrity which can never be taken from me.

PASTORS AND LEADERSHIP

There are many leadership types I could discuss, but I will focus on two relative to pastors and the church. Let's take a look:

Man appointed leaders claim a call from God, but their call is by the authority of human vessels who do not solely speak as directed by the Lord. These leaders are common; they rely on their strength and ability in the areas of academics and formal and informal training. Education is good, but it cannot replace the call of God, which facilitates the anointing. The current church does not need man-made, man-called, or man-trained leadership, because these view ministry as a profession, much like dentistry, fire fighters, police offices, lawyers, judges, or politicians. Man does not choose ministry, God does. Because one can speak multiple languages, pass historical or religious examinations, and are eloquent of speech doesn't make them automatically qualified for the work of ministry. God is sovereign and qualifies all. God alone possesses the power to assign his anointing and authority of the Holy Spirit to manifest fruit and change lives through Jesus Christ.

God Appointed Leaders function in a specific, specialized capacity. In Hebrew, the word appoint means to oversee, to care for; to watch over. Such examples: The appointment of Levites - *Numbers 1:50*; The appointment of Aaron and his sons to the Priesthood – *Numbers 3:10*; The appointment of David as King of Israel – *II Samuel 6:21*; The appointment of the chief Levites as minstrels – *I Chronicles 15:16*; The singers – Heman, Asaph, and Ethan, players of the cymbals of brass – *I Chronicles 15:17-19*; Joshua appointment as the successor of Moses – *Numbers 27:16-22*; and The appointment of deacons by the apostles – *Acts 6:3*.

The objective of the devil is to destroy church leadership. If he can disrupt or destroy leadership, then the church could potentially be thrown into disorder. He starts at the head, displacing pastors and other leaders, before attacking parishioners. Each member must be cautious about their connections, because some within the congregation have been sent to deceive and distract. The book of Nehemiah provides us with a great example of good leadership. He was a leader of influence. (The position pastors occupy is one of influence.) If you say you're leading, then the people should be behind and not in front of you. If this is not the case, you are not a leader. In order to lead you must have followers. Nehemiah questioned the welfare of the people in Jerusalem. He was told that the walls surrounding the city were in ruins; the people were weary, disheartened and very depressed.

This motivated Nehemiah to act, and he responded with tears and prayer. He petitioned God on the behalf of others. He was motivated to protect the people. We should bear one another's burdens *Galatians 6:2* This is where most miss it. Many times, we are so busy fighting one another that we forget we are doing the work of the kingdom. We sit back and wait for others to fail. And we must be careful about our connections. Some will attempt to make you think they're on your side but are not. They will try to pull you away from your God-given assignment, by attending conferences and other church events to distract you from the mission of God. Do as God has directed and no more. If you are a pastor and you are unaware of the needs of the people within your community, my question to you is "What has God called you to?"

Why would the Lord set you in a community without giving you the knowledge to reach the people living there? If all you do is preach on Sunday and go home, the potential of your assignment is limited. Where is your heart for the people and what is your motivation? What drives your actions? There was a time when I saw a need for leaders to come together when I served as pastor. I tried to get other pastors to work together and put their denominational differences aside. Without fail, every time we talked about doing something, there was the attempt to come up with a name for the group. I would always ask why we simply could not work together as believers. Why wasn't it enough to be people of holiness, godly people working together with one purpose? Why do we always have to come up with a name? We make up names like, "Believers of the Westside," or "A New Beginning." We should remember God has not changed, and his assignment is always clear.

In every church I have served as Pastor, I have gone into the community and scouted out the land. I searched to understand the needs of the people, and how I, as the local pastor, could help meet those needs. This was the approach of Nehemiah. Love was his motivator and it was also mine as I knocked on doors and spoke with many. I remember one family in particular: I knocked on their door and the mother of several children answered as I introduced myself as a new pastor in the city. I told her where I was and invited her to church. She told me the family did not have clothes for church, and I reached into my pocket and gave her all I had. I didn't know if she would come to church or not, but I knew she had a need. My objective was to meet the people where they were. On Sunday, while we were in service, I looked up and saw her along with her children. She became a faithful member of the church from that day forward and brought other family members to join as well. I watched God transform her life.

When we look at things through our eyes, we see defeat, lies, and all kinds of disappointments. Similar to the man at the cemetery, people saw his lunacy, bound with shackles and chains, and no one was able to tame him. People branded him by what they saw. Society had deemed him unreachable and worthless, but this man was a diamond in the rough. *Matthew 8:28-34; Mark 5:1-20; and Luke 8:26-39* God does not use good people. You say you're bad, but God sees you as good: Adam ate the forbidden fruit; God told Abraham to leave everything, but he took Lot; Joseph was an arrogant dreamer; Moses a murderer; Gideon fearful; Samson disobedient; Saul unfit to be King; Peter denied Jesus; Judas betrayed Jesus; and Paul was a notorious serial killer. God uses all kinds of people because his calling is not based upon our ability, but rather our availability. And when you are willing to let go of everything, you are then ready to walk in the will of God. *Romans 12:1-2*

Nehemiah carried the needs to the Lord in prayer and God responded. He was given permission from the King to return to his homeland and rebuild the shattered walls of Jerusalem. Despite oppositions from both inside and outside sources, they completed the task in fifty-two days under Nehemiah's leadership. When Nehemiah petitioned God, God gave him everything he needed to rebuild the wall. I love it! When Nehemiah arrived in Jerusalem, for three days he got up in the night and took a few men with him. He told no one about the things God had placed upon his heart. Sometimes, you cannot tell others what you're doing, because the potential for strife, jealousy, and envy exists to deter your plans. Sometimes the people you surround yourself with do not have your best interest at heart. They give an illusion but are inwardly awaiting your downfall.

In the book of Nehemiah, this was true of Sanballat. Sanballat and Geshem sent a message to Nehemiah requesting a meeting. They conspired to do harm against Nehemiah, but Nehemiah responded saying, *I am doing a great work, so that I cannot come down: why should the work cease, whilst I leave it, and come down to you? Nehemiah 6:3b* Sanballat repeated this request four times, and each time Nehemiah answered in the same. Don't be pulled away from your assignment when you know what God has told you. Pastors, I challenge you to be like Jesus. Ask the people you serve, "Who do men say that I am?" After reading this about Jesus, I did the same to those I served. I asked the people to be honest and tell me the truth. This information could help me in areas I could improve. I know Holy Spirit leads and guides, but we are also helpers of one another. Be open to learn about how you are perceived in the community? Take a hard look at the impact you have made and be willing to make improvements.

If your church is receiving upward of twelve thousand dollars every Sunday, and suddenly the contributions stop, a good leader would call a meeting or make other inquiries to understand what has happened. It would be imperative to learn why people change their giving and why the decline has occurred. As a good leader, you would not allow months to pass before understanding the problem. We should be the same when we see souls are not being converted. Why would we sit in our church, month after month, and not question the lack of soul winning, changed lives, or lack of repentance? Why don't we call meetings to ask what is going on? Unfortunately, money has become more important than souls. Jesus commanded us to go into the harvest. We are to compel men to come to salvation.

Matthew 9:35-38 – *And Jesus went about all the cities and villages, teaching in their synagogues, and preaching the gospel of the kingdom, and healing every sickness and every disease among the people. But when he saw the multitudes, he was moved with compassion on them, because they fainted,* *and were scattered abroad, as sheep having no shepherd. Then saith he unto his disciples, The harvest truly is plenteous, but the labourers are few; Pray ye therefore the Lord of the harvest, that he will send forth labourers into his harvest.*

Luke 10:2 – *Therefore said he unto them, The harvest truly is great, but the labourers are few: pray ye therefore the Lord of the harvest, that he would send forth labourers into his harvest.*

Luke 14:23 – *And the lord said unto the servant, Go out into the highways and hedges, and compel them to come in, that my house may be filled.*

Take notice how Jesus saw the multitude and was moved with compassion. The people were weary and scattered like sheep having no shepherd. Pastors, are we conducting ourselves as shepherds, demonstrating compassion for sheep? I am motivated by love, and if you do not love the people of God, you'll never experience divine harvest. Those truly called to the pastorate will go into the harvest, and with compassion, compel others to come to Jesus. The harvest is still ripe. And the answer to their needs are in your mouth.

People come to church for different reasons: Some come because they want to count the offering, but once that has been accomplished, you don't see them anymore till church has ended. They have missed the entire purpose for coming. They've counted the money, but their spirit had not been fed. You may have deacons who attempt to control everything. They want to get up and try to teach without God gifting them to teach. This is not an indictment to all preachers, but something must be said about the state of the church, pastors and other leaders. Adam messed up in the Garden of Eden when he failed to speak out. God addressed his error of say nothing and listening to his wife.

Again, I ask where are the apostles of today? Many say they are apostles, but their focus is on the title more than the assignment. Carrying the title of apostle, bishop, prophet, and pastor in name only is deceitful, and preaching messages without biblical reference is worse. Instead of preaching the gospel, many are preaching "feel good" messages like prosperity, but there is no such thing within the scripture. I'm reminded of a time when I went to church where the pastor told everyone to hold their hands up. I immediately had a flashback from my neighborhood as a kid. When we heard "hold your hands up" we knew a robbery was about to occur. I was robbed without a pistol that Sunday and following church I had to borrow money to get lunch.

So, I say this with love, if you go to a church and the pastor tells you to put your hands up, call 911. Somebody's getting ready to be robbed! There is no such thing as a "Prosperity Gospel." I believe the Bible instructs us to give, so let me highlight a few: The woman with the alabaster box, *Luke 7:37-38*; The poor widow woman who gave all she had, *Luke 21:1-4*; and The believers had all things common – selling their possessions and distributing to others as they had need, *Acts 2:44-46*. In Biblical times, the apostles spoke the same thing. They worked as a unit, wrote letters to the church, and served together. This is not happening today. We have many brothers who say they are Apostles, but where are the ones that the Bible spoke of? The first apostles wrote to the church at Ephesus, Corinth, Galatia, Thessalonica, and others, to name a few.

Today's apostleship is more concerned with the title rather than the assignment. Where are the true men of God? Those truly called are making sure the church is in compliance with the Word of God. The Apostle Paul exhort his son in the ministry, I charge thee therefore before God, and the Lord Jesus Christ, who shall judge the quick and the dead at his appearing and his kingdom; Preach the word; be instant in season, out of season; reprove, rebuke, exhort with all longsuffering and doctrine. For the time will come when they will not endure sound doctrine; but after their own lusts shall they heap to themselves teachers, having itching ears; And they shall turn away their ears from the truth, and shall be turned unto fables. But watch thou in all things, endure afflictions, do the work of and evangelist, make full proof of thy ministry.

Preachers, pastors, evangelists, bishops, and church leaders, these are the times we're living in. May we be aware and preach the Word of God – sound doctrine and not doctrine of men. Stand up for truth and be accountable to God. You may be disliked and abandon by some, and others will refuse to listen, but we have been forewarned by God through our forerunner, Brother Timothy. *And they shall turn away their ears from the truth, and shall be turned unto fables. I Timothy 4:4.* Isaiah commands, *Cry aloud, spare not, lift up thy voice like a trumpet, and shew my people their transgression, and the house of Jacob their sins. Isaiah 58:1.* This is not achievable without committing to the instructions of Apostle Paul: *I beseech you therefore, brethren, by the mercies of God, that ye present your bodies a living sacrifice, holy, acceptable unto God, which is your reasonable service. And be not conformed to this world: but be ye transformed by the renewing of your mind, that ye may prove what is that good, and acceptable, and perfect, will of God. Romans 12:1-2*

Pastors, we do not belong to ourselves any longer. We are God's and must preach the Word of God, feed his sheep, and take care of His children. If we mislead them in anyway, their blood is on our hands. We must refuse to misrepresent God and His House and commit to teach and preach about those things God hates. The church does not belong to anyone but God. Take care of it. No one should have their names plastered all over God's church. The reason I didn't was because people already knew me. I didn't have my name on busses, vans, or any life size images. You know there's a problem when you walk into churches and one of the first things you see is an erected image of the pastor standing six feet tall. The church is not your house, it's the Lord's.

Now the Spirit speaketh expressly, that in the later times some shall depart from the faith, giving heed to seducing spirits, and doctrines of devils; Speaking lies in hypocrisy; having their conscience seared with a hot iron; I Timothy

4:1-2 This is the dilemma of our time. Look at how we have changed the church. We don't hear preaching about adultery, drugs, or homosexuality. We are quiet about nearly everything. We are fearful of causing an offense; therefore, preachers are steering away from enforcing what the Bible says. Pastors are people pleasers, avoiding topics that will upset others. They are nonconfrontational and avoid speaking out for what's right! If it doesn't benefit them, they remain silent. Preachers used to be called names because they preached the Word of God and went against the popularity. We have changed, and the church doesn't look the same.

We have lost a fear of God. People clearly plot against the will of God. They boldly admit that they are not about God. They want to control and dictate to others, but I am not for sale. I remember going to a well-attended church, where the pastor said, "Let me tell you what we are going to do. We will receive a love offering for you and pass out these envelopes as well. Everything in the envelopes is yours..." I stopped and told him he did not have to do that for me. And the reason I said, "I am not a whore. You can't buy me. I'm not for sale." This is what has helped me all my life. I do not preach for money. If you give me something, give it to me. If you don't, I'm fine. I used to tell the church, "You don't have to give me nothing. I'm not allowing you to control me with nothing."

God uniquely made me, and I can't be bought with money. Because I'm this way, I can go in and preach the Word without being controlled by anyone, and I can preach the Word of God without sugar coating it. Don't get upset with me but show me where I'm wrong from the scriptures. Success is not determined by the crowd or size of your church. Although, your church keeps growing it doesn't mean you are successful. Remember, everyone who surrounded Jesus wasn't for him. Many were with him to hear him, but not everyone heeded his words. Because some come to your church doesn't mean they are coming for you. In my young days, I used to go to church, not to hear the preacher, but to see what "that gal" was saying.

There are a lot of young brothers just starting in ministry and don't want to listen to anyone. If you are a pastor or have been called into ministry, and nothing has happened within three years, it is a good indication that God has not called you. If you are a pastor, and you don't have a keen knowledge about your community and you say God called you, it's a good indication that God has not called you. And if you are a pastor but uncompassionate and insensitive to sheep, then it's a good indicator that God did not call you. Those whom God called has a heart for his people. His pastors are compassionate and will leave the 99 to look for one lost. *Matthew 18:10-14; Luke 15:1-7*

SUMMARY

    Leaders of the Lord's church have been given authority in Jesus name to preach the Word of God and win souls. And every believer must understand the operation, under which, this authority exists. Jesus went to hell, in my name, so I can go to heaven in His name. As we walk in authority of Jesus Christ, the Bible states, *Behold, I give unto you power to tread on serpents and scorpions, and over all the power of the enemy: and nothing shall by any means hurt you; Luke 10:19* We have been given power to preach God's Word, and we are further instructed by Paul's letter to the church at Ephesus: *Finally, my brethren, be strong in the Lord, and in the power of His might. Ephesians 6:10* This authority is secured as we equip ourselves with the whole armor of God.

    In the past, I have heard others say, "I need to work on my relationship with God." My response to the statement is "If you don't have a relationship with God, then you have a relationship with Satan." You are working on one relationship or the other. Ask yourself, "Who am I?" If you are teaching things in the church and it does not align with the Word of God, you are wrong, and your teachings are erroneous. The Word of God can't simply be changed because it's a new day or the times are different. The Bible says that Jesus is the same, yesterday, today, and forever more; he remains the same. We have permitted so much to occur in our churches without any biblical grounds. We have our computers, smart phones, and we rarely communicate with one another. We text each other, even if we are sitting at the same table or in the same room of the house. We Are Disconnected and Don't Even Know It!

Operating within God's Will sustains our connection. This means making God's Word a top priority; making him first. This is accomplished by doing the following: 1) Meditating on the Word of God; (2) Putting the Word of God into practice; (3) Developing a habit of making the Word of God first daily; and (4) Obeying the voice of the Spirit of God. If you continually fill your mind with God's Word, you will respond to circumstances accordingly, rather than from your emotions. There are no biblical grounds for women pastors, preachers, apostles, evangelists, bishops or first ladies. God has not called a woman to any role in his church that usurps authority over the man.

Men are putting their daughters and wives in positions of headship and God did not do this. If you love people, love them enough to tell them the truth. Since writing this book, a dear friend, who was like a brother to me passed away. I love him very much. As he battled his illness, I wanted to be there for him, but I would not sit with him in his misery and dwell on unfortunate circumstance. During this time, I was reminded of the man by the pool of Bethesda who waited to be healed. He had his infirmity for thirty-eight years, but when Jesus saw him, he asked, "Do you want to be made whole?" The man replied with excuses. Jesus already knew his condition, and he simply wanted the man to answer "yes" or "no." *John 5:1-15*

We should avoid constant talk about our misery. I talked to my friend; he understood I was not going to sit in his misery with him. And, despite my choice, he knew I still loved him. I continued to encourage him, pray with him, and remind him that he was loved. We tolerate too much. Most will sit and listen at length to stuff that they cannot change, and in the end, it doesn't make anyone feel better. So, I encouraged him with the Word of God and good fellowship. Many times, parents tolerate their children's bad behavior. During the time I was living with my mother, I came home one day to find she had packed my bags and placed them by the front door. Because I would not follow her rules, she forced me to get out of her house.

I found an apartment, and for many years remained away until I began to view life from a different perspective. I realized I wasn't prepared to leave home, so when I went back; I repented to my mom for my past behaviors. I told her I was wrong and promised if she allowed me back, she would never have to worry about me doing the same again. She told me, and I quote, "You can come back, but ain't nothing changed. This is still my house." Anything tolerated is doubtful to change. My mom refused to tolerate my behavior and it forced me to change. In my latter years, I better understood how much God graced me through times when hell broke through on me. I went through stuff and wondered why no one came through to check on me? I checked on others, but they didn't do the same.

I would go to school and check on other parent's children. These kids did not call their parents, they called me. And I also told their parents I had them. I've visited jails and supported people in court: young and old. I defended people and won every case. God gave me favor for His children. It wasn't me. I've helped people get jobs, connect with Goodwill Industries to gain training, and even helped some to get through college. I would go to ESR to help some find jobs and assist others at the Housing Authority to secure apartments or other forms of housing. But when I began going through personal issues or crisis, and all hell broke loose there were few that helped me. I remember one person, Ronald Ramseur, when he heard what I was going through he came to see me. I thank God for him today. I thought family members, or somebody would come by and check on me, but they didn't when I was going through some of the roughest times in my life. I wondered why?

To them, it looked like I had failed. Some were happy. Even when my marriages ended, I don't remember anyone coming to talk or encourage me. It took God to show me. I asked the Lord why didn't people come and check on me? After all of the help I gave to others, no one asked me how I was doing. The Lord allowed me to see that he had made me this way. He told me, "They were not made like you. You were designed and made to go through this." I said so be it and turned my life over into his hands.

I didn't understand when stuff started hitting me. God allowed me to understand whenever anyone is tearing down Satan's kingdom, he will come against you. If Satan attacked Jesus, he's going to do the same against you. God anointed you to do what you do. So, I stopped complaining and realized that although I lost everything, I actually lost nothing. I'm still rolling today. Schools still call me, and I'm still helping people and churches. My calling hasn't changed because it's something God called me to. I thank God for His grace and mercy. It's not about titles: Saying I'm a pastor or bishop. I'm a servant of the Lord. It's not what people call you, but it's the question of can God trust you?

The Lord showed me that being a pastor is like a daycare: people bring their children and trust you to care for them. This what I did when I was a pastor: our church was a kind of daycare. We didn't ask people to come, but when they came, we took care of them. I was the servant of the Lord. It was not about the title, but it was the work of the title. I had to show God He could trust me.

2 Chronicles 7:14 – If My people, which are called by My name, shall humble themselves, and pray, and seek my face, and turn from their wicked ways; then will I hear from heaven, and will forgive their sin, and will heal their land.

This is the Word of God for the people of God. Those who have an ear to hear, let them hear, and Ye that are holy, be holy still. Make sure you are not one of the many. If you are an apostle, be sure of the message you are giving to endorse order in the church. When people talk about leadership you often hear words like power, influence, and leverage. Leaders are people who make things happen. When Jesus spoke of leaders and leadership, we hear words like compassion, humility, gentleness generosity, patience, and service. The Holy spirit makes things happen. A good leader will receive instructions and correction. When you are unable to receive correction, you are not a leader.

I've had people around me who were not good followers: People quick to anger and easy to upset because they possessed a rebellious spirit. People who rejected correction. Like a marriage, when you tell your spouse something God has shown you, and they fight you because of their carnal minds. Remember, (For the weapons of our warfare are not carnal, but mighty through God to the pulling down of strong holds:) *II Corinthians 10:4* It's bad when others tell you they don't care what the Bible says. There's no denying you are dealing with a rebellious spirit. I say to every pastor, come back to the original call of God. Keep in mind, we have been called by God to be salt and light.

Matthew 5:13-16 – *Ye are the salt of the earth: but if the salt have lost his savour, wherewith shall it be salted? It is thenceforth good for nothing, but to be cast out, and to be trodden undo foot of men.*

Today, the tragedy is not that sinners' sin, because that's what they do, but the church as a whole has failed to act as salt and light in our society. Ever since man's fall, we were born in sin and shaped in iniquity. Although you can find a church on nearly every corner, our communities continue to be destroyed by violence, poverty, despair, and selfishness. Things have become more important than people. Christ told us, *This know also, that in the last days perilous times shall come. For men shall be lovers of their own selves, covetous, boasters, proud, blasphemers, disobedient to parents, unthankful, unholy, without natural affection, trucebreakers, false accusers, incontinent, fierce, despisers of those that are good, traitors, heady, highminded, lovers of pleasures more than lovers of God; II Timothy 3:1-4*

Paul admonishes us, *I charge thee therefore before God, and the Lord Jesus Christ, who shall judge the quick and the dead at his appearing and his kingdom; Preach the word; be instant in season, out of season; reprove, rebuke, exhort with all longsuffering and doctrine. II Timothy 4:1-2* I repeat it again, Pastors and leaders, we are living in the time when men are not enduring sound doctrine. People are heaping to themselves teachers with itching ears and running after the lust of their own hearts. Our nation has turned away from the truth, but our calling remains the same. Do you remember when you had a zeal for the Lord? You woke up excited and wanted to tell everybody about the Lord. You witnessed and prayed for people simply because God saved you. Your objective was to win the lost at any cost. Our objective is still the same today. We are called to be soul winners!

Many have claimed to know God or His Will, but I want to leave you in closing with the following scriptures: *II*

Corinthians 4:1-16 and *Isaiah 55:6-11*. Paul warns the church, pastors and leaders alike to not mishandle the Word of God. We need to clearly understand that the ministry itself has been received from God with mercy – we must not faint or change it in any way to satisfy our needs. He tells us to renounce hidden things of dishonesty, refrain from handling the word of God deceitfully, but to walk in truth. Isaiah 55:11 tells us that the Word of God will never return to Him void or unfulfilled. As believers, each of us needs to seek the Lord while He may be found. (Say and do only as God has said and left on record in his Word.) *Let the wicked forsake his way, and the unrighteous man his thoughts: and let him return unto the Lord, and he will have mercy upon him; and to our God, for he will abundantly pardon. For my thoughts are not your thoughts, neither are your ways my ways, saith the Lord. Isaiah 55:7-8*

The Word of God for the people of God! Amen.

www.ingramcontent.com/pod-product-compliance
Lightning Source LLC
Chambersburg PA
CBHW070444090426
42735CB00012B/2462